A South Carolina Requiem

A South Carolina Requiem

TONY SCULLY

RESOURCE *Publications* · Eugene, Oregon

A SOUTH CAROLINA REQUIEM

Resource Publications
An Imprint of Wipf and Stock Publishers
199 W. 8th Ave., Suite 3
Eugene, OR 97401

www.wipfandstock.com

PAPERBACK ISBN: 978–1-6667–3677–9
HARDCOVER ISBN: 978–1-6667–9556–1
EBOOK ISBN: 978–1-6667–9557–8

FEBRUARY 18, 2022 11:41 AM

To John Shelby Spong

1931–2021

In his many books and writings Bishop Spong, a voice of liberation,
has revealed the foundation texts of Scripture,
both Old and New Testaments,
as poetry to be questioned, explored, and celebrated.

You shine within us, outside us—even darkness shines—when we remember

—The Lord's Prayer, translated from the Aramaic

Contents

PERMISSIONS

Professor Edward Ayers of the University of Richmond has granted permission for the use of his quotation about Southern identity in the Introduction.

For the scripture texts, I chose The American Standard Version (ASV) for its language and its remarkable history. The ASV is in universal public domain. The traditional hymns and spirituals are also in universal public domain, as are the traditional prayers of the Requiem Mass.

For *The Backcountry*, the introductory quotation is in the public domain. Cf. https://teachingamericanhistory.org/library/document/the-journal-of-reverand-charles-woodmason/

For *Mary Boykin Chesnut*, the quotation in the introduction is from *A Diary from Dixie*, Mary Boykin Chesnut, 1823–1886 (Public domain. Cf. Project Gutenberg)

For *John Lewis*, the quotation in the introduction is from *Across That Bridge: Life Lessons and a Vision for Change* (2012, public library)

For *President Obama*, regarding the introduction, public speeches of Presidents are in the public domain

Two poems in this text, *Psalm 18* and The Kaddish (*Give Thanks to the Jews)* are from *A Carolina Psalter* by Tony Scully (Wipf and Stock 2019)

A South Carolina Requiem, by Anthony Patrick Scully, is registered with the Library of Congress. Registration Number: TXu 2–291–995 (November 30, 2021)

PREFACE

A South Carolina Requiem celebrates the power of a resilient and courageous people.

A South Carolina Requiem, the final book in his trilogy, evokes Tony Scully's earlier books, *A Carolina Psalter* (Wipf & Stock, 2019) and *Come into the Light* (Wipf & Stock, 2020), with poems addressing foundation texts with questions and occasional confrontation as we move into new understandings of Spirit.

As South Carolina strives forward in cultural achievements in science, education, and the arts, *A South Carolina Requiem* celebrates the warmth of its people, and their continuing determination for justice and civil rights.

A South Carolina Requiem acknowledges the struggles over the centuries of dirt farmers and mill workers, the removal of the Cherokee in the Trail of Tears, and the injustices of slavery and Jim Crow as the threshold to rebirth and transformation.

Scully's poems interact with South Carolina traditions and rituals: the Baptist hymns; the Presbyterian hymns; Anglican hymns; the Kaddish; the Cherokee prayer at death; significant sermons in the history of the Carolinas; and the Requiem Mass, itself a compendium of ancient and revered texts. The poems also interact with the sometimes controversial public events and personalities that have challenged and ultimately transformed the people of the state.

Acknowledgements

Thank you to the following people for their assistance with the publication of *A South Carolina Requiem*: to my late wife, Joy Claussen Scully, for her constant support, humor, and love over thirty-seven years; to Richard Brown, Director of the University of South Carolina Press, for his friendship and encouragement; to my late friend, the deeply-missed Reverend Dr. William F. ("Chip") Summers for his near-infinite wisdom and unfailing sense of humor in all matters secular and profane; to Marty Daniels, a light-keeper, for her unerring eye and abiding judgment; to Earl Bryant, MD for his sense of reality after a lifetime of practicing pediatric medicine; to Drew Casper, PhD, professor emeritus and legend at the University of Southern California School of Cinematic Arts, a close friend since we were teenagers, for his enthusiasm for my work, even for my worst instincts; to Nina ffrench-Frazier von Eckardt, artist and critic extraordinaire; to Ponza and Robert Vaughan; Kitty and Henry Beard; Ken and Boo DuBose; Mike and Marlene Mischner; and Tanya and Bob Artinian, the best of friends; and especially to Herb Martin for his critical eye, and for his six decades of being there for me.

INTRODUCTION

SOUTH Carolina, an arena of numerous indigenous civilizations over the millennia, beginning about 500 years ago became a landing ground for European explorers, expatriates, and immigrants fleeing wars and persecution. During these early years, this brave new world for Europeans often proved to be a place of darkness for the native populations, as well as for the enslaved peoples transported here against their will. In recent generations, with new arrivals from Latin America, Africa, and Asia, South Carolina has become an increasingly emblematic presence in the international landscape. Like most regions with complex histories, this state is open to interpretation, and probably because of those histories, to multi-faceted conversations about its relative importance in the world community.

With archeological explorations continuing, future generations will hopefully treasure the contributions of the indigenous cultures—the Cherokee (Iroquoian), Saluda (Algonquin), Edisto and Yemassee (Muskogean), and the Wateree, Congaree, and other Mississippian people who came together to become the Catawba Nation. In the meantime, one can hope we will listen carefully to the voices of the native spirit traditions and to their wisdom about the land and the animals. In time, the influence of our embedded Africa civilizations here will also become of greater consequence, especially how the presence of Islam in a high percentage of the enslaved, however suppressed, has fed into our sense of the holy. So too, ensuing generations will continue to honor African Americans taking the moral high ground in leading the nation into a greater awareness of social justice. In its ever-developing character, South Carolina, like most of the country, is increasingly recognizing the incoming Hispanic traditions, especially the Mexican, with all the complexities of that country's inherent Mesoamerican inheritance. By degrees, the present Anglo-Saxon, Anglo-Celtic, and Germanic ascendancy are incorporating this new world. We are from the start Mississippi, Muskogean, Anglo-Saxon, Celt, Norman, Polish, Slovak, Russian, and a veritable carnival of arrivals from Barbados, China, Syria, Somalia, Sweden, Italy, Guatemala, Poland, Sierra Leone, the Congo, Nigeria, Kenya, Sri Lanka, Vietnam—in short, the people of Planet Earth. Clearly, with this pronounced movement of populations and philosophies, our continuing narrative is real enough—and riveting.

How southern, then, is this "South" with which Southerners identify? Many of the people in South Carolina, one discovers, descend at least in part from parents and grandparents from northern states; ancestors from the Plymouth Colony are not unusual. So too, many of the Confederates were the children and grandchildren of immigrants. The paternal grandfather of Jefferson Davis, President of the Confederacy, as one example, immigrated from Wales; his maternal grandparents in turn immigrated from Ireland and Scotland. The inescapable question persists: in terms of cultural identity, what element then holds the South together? By all accounts, Southern identify is remarkably strong—strong enough to die for. To Southerners, the South is everything. Do we know why? The fact is, there's no simple answer. Self-identified Southerners might find the comments of Professor Edward Ayers of the University of Richmond about Southern identity to be particularly enlightening:

> Southern history bespeaks a place that is more complicated than the stories we tell about it. Throughout its history, the South has been a place where poverty and plenty have been thrown together in especially jarring ways, where democracy and oppression, white and black, slavery and freedom, have warred. The very story of the South is a story of unresolved identity, unsettled and restless, unsure and defensive. The South, contrary to so many words written in defense and in attack, was not a fixed, known, and unified place, but rather a place of constant movement, struggle, and negotiation.

I approach South Carolina as someone who grew up in Washington, DC in the fifties when the city was reportedly 70% Black, with most of the African American population in the Capital part of the Great Migration, also known as the Black Migration. About six million Black people emigrated from the South between the end of World War One and 1970. In DC, African Americans generally moved north from states directly south: Virginia, South Carolina, North Carolina, and Georgia. Among the White population, mainly because of the GI bill, many returning veterans, Black and White, also emigrated from those same southern states, escaping what was then the endemic poverty and turbulent politics of the South during the Great Depression.

My late wife, Joy Claussen, a veteran of Broadway musicals and a native of Pittsburgh, and I decided to move to Camden, South Carolina in 2005 after she had performed an evening of Broadway music at the home of attorney Tom Mullikin with his uncle, the performer Bill Mullikin, our longtime friend. The Mullikins, stalwarts of the Camden community, had originally hailed from Baltimore with an endearing mother from North Carolina. They, like us and many others in Camden, came from Catholic backgrounds; some of us are educated Catholics, some not, some practicing Catholics, some not. The religious landscape of South Carolina, as one pivotal index, has been changing along with everything else. In a once predominantly Baptist and Methodist culture, the Mormons are making their mark. Hindus have been growing in numbers and importance. The Jewish presence here, not often acknowledged in popular accounts, has been longstanding and resilient. In short, the various levels of the Southern society are constantly changing, shifting, and accommodating new arrivals. As Professor Ayers points out, the idea of the South as a fixed and immutable place no longer applies.

A South Carolina Requiem is intended to be a love letter to South Carolina and its sometimes complicated, multi-layered history, its many interconnected and often intermarried populations, from the indigenous tribes and the later arrivals of the Europeans: common laborers, farmers, soldiers and, tradesmen. Without doubt, the enslaved are also pivotal to this place. And how could one overlook the remarkable aristocrats who take up so much of the recorded history here?

Why *A South Carolina Requiem*? Why not, *A South Carolina Primer*, or *A South Carolina Celebration*? "Requiem" connotes a lament, a dirge, a funeral song. Why emphasize what at first might sound negative and possibly depressing? Is poetry not supposed to celebrate the wellspring of life itself, of birth, of beauty and song?

In many respects, South Carolina could be described as the heart of the country; it's even shaped like a heart, and like all hearts, sometimes buoyant, and suffused with love, sometimes heavy, ravaged, and betrayed. In its racial history, South Carolina has seen the face of benevolence and the face of rage. In some family histories, the South has proven to be a home of demonstrably warm and welcoming people with a rich cultural memory, from the splendid culinary traditions and the marvelous stories that mark the conversations among friends. Across the country, however, especially with African Americans with South Carolina roots, ancestral memories can be multi-layered: often warm; often bittersweet; and sometimes dark.

Some of the poems in *A South Carolina Requiem* are conversations with the often hard events of the last three hundred years. Other poems sing in response to the prayers and hymns of a buoyant, religious people. One cannot address South Carolina without becoming deeply invested in its faith traditions. The pervasive kindness of believers in small towns and cities across the American South suggests the people here are deeply touched by the Bible, especially by the Jesus of the Gospels. From prayers to "Our Lord and Savior," come armies of compassionate, world-serving people, who in the imitation of Christ serve the homeless, the hungry, the grieving, and the incarcerated with warm hearts and the best of intentions. For many others, however, the Bible sets forth outmoded or impossible absolutes, notably the injunctions about the place of women and slaves. Where to start?

As mayor of a South Carolina city, I spent many hours in many churches, especially at funerals and anniversary services, with congregations praising the name of God. Whatever else, the South remains a culture of hymns and blessings. Those blessings mark us and lift us up. Those blessings also challenge us. As we press forward with our exuberant spirits in this extraordinary place, we also live with ghosts. If we listen carefully, we can hear the shouts and cries from the Indian wars, the American Revolution, the Civil War, and feel the sorrows of the enslaved.

And from every corner we hear praise.

As It Was in the Beginning

The Patron Saint

KING Haigler (c. 1700–1763) was Chief or King of the Catawbas from 1754 to 1763. He negotiated a number of treaties with both North and South Carolina, guaranteeing safety and support for his people and protection for the settlers. His men later fought on the American side in our Revolution. He is known as the patron saint and co-founder of Camden, South Carolina, the oldest city in the midlands.

On August 30, 1763, a band of Shawnees murdered King Haigler. He was the first Native American to be inducted into the South Carolina Hall of Fame.

"Thomas Spratt and King Haigler," charlottetrailofhistory.org

King Haigler
Monarch of our conjurings
You reign over the rest of us
Your bow drawn
Alert
To caw and trill and whispering

You are totem
Icon
Priest of the assembled tribes

Guardian of all that breathes
In the wood
The grasslands
And along the water's edge

We are interlopers
And thieves
More cruel than murderers
We have fenced in your land
Taken your women
And brought disease

Worse
We have commandeered
Your story
And stolen your history

Despite us
You founded our city
And bequeathed to us
The revelation
Of belonging
To this beloved land

Unbeknownst
Even to us
We are your people

In time
We will grow into our inheritance
We will understand the breathing land
We will recognize whom we have become

In that day to come
We will honor you
At last
And pay homage
Even to ourselves

The descendants
Of your soul

The Old Slave Mart

THE Old Slave Mart, at 6 Chalmers Street in Charleston, constructed in 1859, once housed a slave auction house, known as Ryan's Slave Mart, named for City Councilman Thomas Ryan. Auctions were held at the Mart until approximately 1863. The building is believed to be the last remaining slave auction house in South Carolina. In 1975, the building was added to the National Register of Historic Places. Today, it houses the Old Slave Mart Museum.

"Old Slave Mart," Wikipedia

In this panegyric
This eulogy for all we are
We mourn
The deaths of the enslaved
Unknown
Unnamed
Undisclosed

Translation:
Disenfranchised
Dumb
Three-fifths
Of a human being
Grown-up boys and girls
Good for the economy
In the proud plantations
Along the rivers of the South

Or would we rather celebrate
Instead
The cries of
Dark survivors
Dragooned
Garroted
Dragged into
Madness

Who have risen from the dead?

By design
We do not wallow in the dark
We wait

And wait again

Until afterwards

After bloodshed
And violence
After insult and customary hate
The emancipated
One by one
Rise into immortality
And light

How could they not?

Their songs had long since
Assured deliverance
Across the water wide
Bands of angels coming fast
Yes, Ma'am

Huddled masses
Immigrating here
From famine
Pogroms
Peasantry
Arrived at
This breeding ground
Of continents
This unforgiving Black and White
All the while
The descendants of the crucified
Quadroons

Octoroons
Gullah gods
Command the narrative
And lead the way

Onetime strangers
Now in passionate embrace
Procreate
A golden race
Negotiating contradiction
And ambivalence

How could they not?

THE ENTRANCE

O NE cannot address the history and the culture of South Carolina without acknowledging its pervasive faith in God, from blessings at meals, to weddings and funerals, to the everyday prayers of its people. The Mass remains an ancient foundation text that in its traditional passages, from praise, from confession, from the blessings of bread and wine, from remembering the dead, from its statement of belief in God the Father, feeds into the worship rituals of most Christian denominations.

I will go to the altar of God, to God, who giveth joy to my youth.

FROM THE BEGINNING OF THE MASS,
ONCE OMITTED FROM THE REQUIEM MASS, HERE RESTORED.

I will go to the altar of God
To God
Who
Despite religious marketing
And furious intent
Despite doubt
Depression
And too much alcohol
Nevertheless giveth joy to my youth

I go
With questions and complaints
Insisting on the worst of narratives

In spite of myself
Me
An almost but not quite
Perpetual irritant
Asking the meaning
Of this mostly imagined deity

This so-called
Creative source
Worshippers expect
To cure sickness
Create prosperity
Advance careers
Watch over children
And above all
Bless wars

From time immemorial
The inherited divinity
Has ordered the sacrifice
Of virgins
Sheep and goats
Never to discount
Nuns
Priests
And otherwise embezzled lives

To believe in the god of
My ancestors means
Abandoning my mind
Surrendering to platitudes

Please God
Whoever you are
Remember me
My questioning keeps me alive

In the meantime
Beyond mind and thought
We feel the energy of love
That creates the stars
And makes the universe
Examining indeed
The air we breathe
Looking into light

And gravity
And time

I will go to the altar of God
To God who giveth joy to my youth

AMAZING GRACE

A MAZING Grace is a Christian hymn published in 1779, with words written in 1772 by the English poet and Anglican clergyman John Newton (1725–1807).

The opening words, *Amazing grace! How sweet the sound that saved a wretch like me!* reflects John Newton's career as a slave trader. He'd had a near-death experience, when his slave ship was almost destroyed in a violent storm, inspiring him to convert to Christianity. Deborah Carlton Loftis, executive director of the Hymn Society in the United States and Canada, says the hymn wasn't popular in England, but became popular in the United States during the Second Great Awakening in the early 1800s when thousands of people, White and Black, gathered for revival meetings.

"Amazing Grace," Wikipedia

Amazing Grace, How sweet the sound
That saved a wretch like me
I once was lost, but now am found
T'was blind but now I see
T'was Grace that taught my heart to fear
And Grace, my fears relieved
How precious did that grace appear
The hour I first believed
Through many dangers, toils and snares
We have already come.
T'was grace that brought us safe thus far
And grace will lead us home

Is grace amazing
Or does it pour down like rain
And swim in the blood
And rivers run?

A wretch like me?

According to the text
Is this for real
Or for rhetorical effect?

Lost
Blind
Deaf and dumb
Nobody saves me
From nothin'

We don't get saved
From dangers
Toils
And snares
We descend into the dark
Drowning in the screams
Of monsters

Or are those voices merely us?

We are savaged
Wrecked
And torn apart
And only then
Will we hear the voice within
That whispers
We are home

Who said how sweet the sound?
Sweetness comes in the spring
The wash of plenitude
The gurgling of the newly born

Only afterwards
Only then
Will we meet the challenges
Of why we arrived
At this god-forsaken plain

Of loss and unknowing

Only afterwards

Only then
Will we understand
The god within

T'was Grace that taught my heart to fear?

Did I not always fear?
And still do fear
Despite entreaties day and night
I am yet composed of terror
Dread
Alarm
Thunder and lightning that comes too close
Police with dogs
The Klan
Afraid of the knock in the middle of the night
And the rock through the window

I've given up waiting to be found
Who would find me
When
And what would they do?

And who would they be
But me
Once again
Looking for myself

Not understanding
The power
The grace
The me

Is one

GULLAH

THE Gullah are African Americans in the low country of Georgia, Florida, South Carolina, and North Carolina, in both the coastal plain and the Sea Islands. They developed a culture with a pervasive African influence.

The Gullah people and their language are also called Geechee, possibly derived from the Ogeechee River near Savannah, Georgia. *Gullah* is a term that originally designated the creole dialect of English spoken by Gullah and Geechee people. Over time, its speakers have used this term to refer to their creole language and distinctive ethnic identity.

"Gullah," Wikipedia

We are
Fulani
Mandinka
Fante
Ashanti
Yoruba
Congos
Angola
Ibos
Coromantees
Guineas
We are black light
Brilliant
Over the majesty
Of sea and sky
We shine with the glory of Africa
On the Carolina coast
We are the gift given
To the emerging lands of the Americas
We are the gathering of worlds
Holding in ourselves
The ancient sounds of humankind

We are Gullah and Geechee

Some day you will understand
How we are you

Swing Low, Sweet Chariot

Coming for to carry me home
Swing low, sweet chariot
Coming for to carry me home

I looked over Jordan and what did I see
Coming for to carry he home
A band of angels coming after me
Coming for to carry me home

Swing low, sweet chariot
Coming for to carry me home
Swing low, sweet chariot
Coming for to carry me home

If you get there before I do
Coming for to carry me

TRADITIONAL SPIRITUAL

A band of angels
Two trombones
A trumpet
And a saxophone
Coming for to carry me home
To the promised land
Of jazz
And jambalaya

How could Heaven
Surrender
Sweet sounds
And the taste of holy trinity?

Why abandon beauty
For mere vibration
High
How high?
And the vision of a deity

If you get there
Before I do
Come to me
In my dreams
And tell me Heaven
Can be fun
Maybe even delicious
Maybe
Everyone we have come to love
Awaits us there

Or is "Heaven"
Code for freedom
Is that it?
From deprivation
And suffering?

And growing old

We await the angels

Please come anytime

Anytime at all

The Backcountry

CHARLES Woodmason was an Anglican clergyman remembered for his journal, *The Carolina Backcountry on the Eve of the Revolution*. Woodmason documented life in the upstate, then the American frontier, in the late 1760s. As he saw it, immorality, if not social chaos, appeared to be the norm. After a few weeks in Pinetree, later renamed Camden, the oldest city in the Midlands, he wrote,

> *The people around, of abandon'd Morals, and profligate Principles - Rude - Ignorant - Void of Manners, Education or Good Breeding - No genteel or Polite Person among them - The people are of all Sects and Denominations - a mix'd medley from all Countries and the Off Scouring of America.* Lowcountry aristocracy fared little better; Woodmason described them as *haughty, frivolous, and domineering.*

Woodmason wrote further:

> "*Most of these People had never before seen a Minister, or heard the Lords Prayer, Service or Sermon in their Days. They were as rude in their Manners as the Common Savages, and hardly a degree removed from them. Their Dresses almost as loose and Naked as the Indians, and differing in Nothing save Complexion. Nakedness is not censurable or indecent here, and they expose themselves often quite Naked, without Ceremony—Rubbing themselves and their Hair with Bears Oil and tying it up behind in a Bunch like the Indians— being hardly one degree removed from them—In few Years, I hope to bring about a Reformation, as I already have done in several Parts of the Country*
>
> *Hence it is that above 30,000£ Sterling have lately been expended to bring over 5 or 6000 Ignorant, mean, worthless, beggarly Irish Presbyterians, the Scum of the Earth, and Refuse of Mankind, I would not wish my worst Enemy to come to this Country . . . to combat perpetually with Papists, Sectaries, Atheists and Infidels— who would rather see the Poor People remain Heathens and Ignorants, than to be brought over to the Church. Such Enemies to Christ and his Cross, are these vile Presbyterians.*

"THE BACKCOUNTRY," TEACHINGAMERICANHISTORY.ORG

Charles Woodmason
A proud
Imperious
Divinely anointed
Bitch

Nevertheless
According to him
This well-intentioned
Educated clergyman
C of E
On the eve of revolution
Excuse me
Did someone say bigot?
Definitely a dogmatist
Kicks the upcountry Presbyterians
In their collective face
Just as they're getting their second wind

Imagine
The women
Half-undressed
Lingering in log cabins
Hair bear-greased
Unbaptized
Not to mention
No nail polish
Root canals
Botox
Plantation shutters
And God knows
No transactional analysis

Scotch-Irish scum
Never heard of crème fraiche
Chateau Neuf du Pape
Or Aeschylus
What about Napoleons?

No, the dessert
Mille-feuille?
Unpronounceable
Of course

Woodmason demands
These redneck roustabouts
Appreciate
English enterprise
And its well-appointed church
Providing structure
Hierarchy
Doctrine
And ultimately
Artificial birth control

Give in
Presbyterian savages
Surrender
To civilization
Ivory Soap
Penicillin
And fabulous portfolios

Haven't we been through this rigamarole before
With Rome?

How about Washington DC?

How about Berlin 1933?

HERITAGE

Once upon a time
In our Revolutionary War
We fought a battle here

Barefoot boys
Eating unripe corn and dirt
Died for their country
Spitting blood
And brains
Scattered to the winds

Typhoid, dysentery, cholera
Bearing down
Ravaging
Wrecking us
More than guns
And rhetoric

Two hundred years
After the main event
Crowds line up to see
This empty space, this field
Where war had been

Heritage infects the brain
Twisting time and memory
Into primordial myth
We stop the now
With any possible excuse

We sit on sacred land,
At least in the telling
Our dead demand
We end our imaginings

And worship them

Our ancestors in uniform
Remain our gods
And hold our souls

With this connection
We maintain identity

Auld Lang Syne

ROBERT Burns (1759–1796), also known familiarly as Rabbie Burns, was a Scottish poet and lyricist. He is widely regarded as the national poet of Scotland and is celebrated worldwide.

As of 2019, through his five surviving children, Robert Burns, who died at 37, has over 900 living descendants.

"Robert Burns," Wikipedia

Should auld acquaintance be forgot
And never brought to mind?
Should auld acquaintance be forgot
And days of auld lang syne?

For auld lang syne, my dear
For auld lang syne
We'll tak a cup o' kindness yet
For days of auld lang syne

ROBERT BURNS 1788

Rabbie Burns
Up from Ayrshire
How did you get to be Bard
Of all the Scots
Scotch-Irish
Anyone with a hearth
And a self-designated heart?

On the run
From indigence
You call out the grandeur
Of the so-called common man
The crofter
The worker
The yeoman

The hand

You extoll
The ploughman
And praise the plough

In the Carolina upstate here
Hardscrabble land
Of log cabins
Textile mills
Dirt farms
Wholesale resistance to anything imperial

You come to us
The evicted
And the dispossessed
To us
Your own
Carrying cluttered lives
Outside children
Too many dead before their time

You come to lovers
Falling into night
Disconnected
And still wandering

Beloved Bard
You bring the Highlands here
The ground
That underlies the ordinary life
The common earth
The soil that perseveres
Through DNA

And walks through death

Requiem

The Carolinas aren't too much a Catholic place
Ten percent
Statistics say
Used to be two

Hernando DeSoto
Reportedly devout
Arrived here in 1540
Looking for gold
And maybe some Indians to save

Some priest they say
Offered Mass on a mountaintop
No doubt a Requiem
As Conquistadores died of everything
En route to Paradise
Taking with them Cherokee
And Creek

This is my Body
Take ye and eat

Sounds fascinating in a history book
Not so much when you're
A free-thinking Jewish
Anabaptist
Quaker
Muslim
Atheist
Choose one of the above

Forgetting Inquisitions
And religious wars
These days

We bury our dead
With the Kaddish
And the Baptist hymns
The Cherokee chant
The Islamic nawafil
And fragments of the Catholic Mass
Here's to success in the Afterworld

Traditions channel grief
And in our sorrow
Make us one

At least for an afternoon

HUGUENOTS

HUGUENOTS were French Protestants of the Reformed, or Calvinist tradition, beginning in early 16th century France. By 1572, on the eve of the St. Bartholomew Day Massacre, the Huguenots represented almost 10% of the population. By 1600, they had declined to 7 or 8%, and were further reduced with persecution under Louis XIV's Edict of Fontainebleau in 1685.

As Huguenots emigrated from France, they established themselves in many places, including London, Dublin, and Charleston, South Carolina where they frequently intermarried into the local establishment.

"Huguenots," Wikipedia

Who are you Huguenots?
Crawling out from under France
You withstand the Vatican
Versailles
And the ravages of greed

Hold to the gods
That are given to you
No court
No country
Can occupy your mind

You come to Charleston
Dispossessed
Overtaken by intolerance
Haunted by the human dark
Determined to survive the night

As it was in the beginning
Is now
And ever shall be
Yes
You thrive
Forgoing France

Relinquishing the Louis

Prospering in the given light

Merci a Dieu

You're ours!

Kyrie—Lord Have Mercy

Kyrie, eleison
Christe, eleison!
Kyrie, eleison

ORIGINATING IN THE GREEK LITURGY

Lordie Lordie
Have mercy on me
Who am I talking to?
I'm the one
That needs to have mercy on me

For doin' what? Choose one:

1. Getting canned

2. Divorced

3. Caught with my pants down

4. Mama, I was jus' showin' off

5. Cheating the I.R.S. (Not sorry at all)

6. Dyin'

7. That's it

8. That's all there is

Christ, have mercy
Why am I the one who always gets caught?
You could have predicted I'd drop dead
Of course I did
Christ have mercy
Thas what it says
Christ
Sweet man
No bearing on nobody I know

29

Jesus
He died on the tree
Lynched like the rest of us
Stabbed in the heart
Beaten down

You say I'm 'sposed to be like him?
Have mercy on me
Have mercy on the rest of us
No way out
Have mercy
Mercy

Hey

The Trail of Tears

THE Trail of Tears refers to the forced relocations of approximately 60,000 Native Americans from their homes in the southeastern United States to regions west of the Mississippi River designated as Indian Territory. The U.S. Government carried out the relocations with the passage of the Indian Removal Act in 1830. On their march west, the Native Americans suffered from exposure, disease, and starvation; approximately 4,000 died. The removals included members of the Chickasaw, Choctaw, Creek, Seminole, and Cherokee people, including Black slaves who lived among them. The Cherokee removal in 1838, the last forced removal, was brought on by the discovery of gold in Georgia, resulting in the Georgia Gold Rush. Approximately 2,000–8,000 of the 16,543 relocated Cherokee died along the way.

"Trail of Tears," Wikipedia

Two thousand
Eight thousand
Will we ever know?

Dead
Diseased
Starved out

Cherokee
Creek
Seminole
Choctaw
Chickasaw
Forcibly removed
From ten thousand years
Of home
Relocated west
By Anglo Saxon
Slaveholding
Life liberty pursuit of happiness
All men are created equal

Regular guys
Holding guns
And bank accounts

Thank you
Andrew Jackson
Slaveholding President
Presiding over cruelty
Son of Irish immigrants
Escaping nightmare
And death
Don't you know better?

The two and a half-year
Japanese internment camps
In World War Two
Get most of the publicity
Just as well
Why remember
Yet another state-supported Hell?

The only good Indian's a dead Indian
Pronounced General in charge of the Army
Philip Sheridan
Famously
Defining savages
His word
Another first generation
Irish American
And Catholic to boot
What was he thinking?
Had he too
Forgotten his own?

Were not the Cherokee
A lost tribe of Israel
One of too many tribes destroyed?
Did they not retaliate

Against waves
Of white barbarians?
Did they not gouge European flesh
To save their race?

When do we grieve?
When do we mourn?

When do we embrace
People other than our own?

CHEROKEE FUNERAL PRAYER

I give you this one thought to keep
I am with you still
I do not sleep
I am a thousand winds that blow
I am the diamond glints on snow
I am the sunlight on ripened grain
I am the gentle autumn rain
When you awaken in the morning's hush
I am the swift, uplifting rush
Of quiet birds in circled flight
I am the soft stars that shine at night
Do not think of me as gone
I am with you still
In each new dawn

ATTRIBUTED TO THE CHEROKEE

We have stopped seeing
Diamond glints on snow
And sunlight on ripened grain

Where is the autumn rain?

We that have eyes to see
Are blind to ourselves
Apparently

Most of us survive
Surveying rhetoric
Electing narcissists
Experts in everything
Except the heart

Where are the soft stars at night?

In the cities
The sky is asphalt

And impenetrable

His Eye Is on the Sparrow

Behold the birds of the heaven, that they sow not, neither do they reap, nor gather into barns; and your heavenly Father feedeth them. Are not ye of much more value then they? (Matthew 6:26) and Are not two sparrows sold for a penny? and not one of them shall fall on the ground without your Father: but the very hairs of your head are all numbered. Fear not therefore: ye are of more value than many sparrows. (Matthew 10:29–31)

I sing because I'm happy
I sing because I'm free
His eye is on the sparrow
And I know He watches me
His eye is on the sparrow
And I know He watches
I know He watches
I know He watches me
I sing because I´m happy
I sing because I´m free
His eye is on the sparrow
And I know He watches me
His eye is on the sparrow
And I know He watches me
He watches me
I know
He watches
Me

BY LYRICIST CIVILLA D. MARTIN
AND COMPOSER CHARLES H. GABRIEL, 1905.

I sing because I'm happy
I sing because I'm free
I am loved
Immeasurably

What about you?

His eye is on the sparrow
The lark
The kangaroo
And every unattended cry
Of baby animals
And newborn kings
Fragile ones
You never heard about
Or knew

He knows the chaos of the day
And the listening of night
He watches everyone they say
Even you and me

Something
To imagine
If you still cannot believe
He watches you
He do
He does
They do too
Spirits lingering between the breaths
Watchers invisible
Unseen

Sparrows tumbled by the millions
Once they blackened out the sky
Buffalo once thundering
Have mostly gone to die

Did he see them too?

Did he watch them fall?

Did you?

Prayers of the Faithful

In the Prayers of the Faithful in the Requiem Mass, the people respond to the word of God, which they have welcomed in faith, and offer prayers for the salvation of all.

In confidence
We invoke God's blessing
To borrow mercy
And discover grace
When we need help
From hemorrhoids
And where did I leave my glasses?

Lord hear our prayer

We pray for the sick and the housebound
Like Aunt May
She lost her leg
Diabetes
And then the rest of her

We give thanks for doctors
Nurses
Caregivers
May we be deaf, dumb, and blind
By the time they carry the silver out of the house
Not to mention my grandmother's engagement ring
From Cartier's
She said
The appraiser said it came from Sears
24 karat glass

Lord, hear our prayer

We pray for those who mourn
May their tears be wiped away

Don't much like bereavement
Don't appreciate despair

Death's coming fast to the rest of us
Like a freight train down the track

Lord hear our prayer

I had to toss my old chaise lounge
The springs were shot
The lady said
Whoever she was
We give thanks for our blessings
Eggs are still cheap

Lord hear our prayer

We pray for the corpse in that coffin
I don't remember his name
May God receive him kindly
With generosity and grace
Forgetting he cheated on taxes
Bludgeoned his wife
And drank himself
Into oblivion

Mother Mary
Intercede for us
And be waiting for us
At the end of our days
To welcome us
Into eternal life

Lord hear our prayer

Hello?

ISLAM

HISTORIANS estimate that as many as 30% of the American enslaved from central African countries like Gambia and Cameroon were Muslim. Among other difficulties they faced, slaves were forced to abandon Islam, both to separate them from their culture and also to "civilize" them to Christianity. Historian Sylviane Diouf chronicles how slaves preserved aspects of their religious traditions and found new ways to express them, by singing in the fields, as one example. Diouf contends that blues music, as another, can track its origins to Muslim influences from the slave period.

Islam, a word that means "surrender" to God, derived from the Arab word for peace, is not a creed in the Western sense. The Muslim bears witness in his actions that his priority is Allah, and that no other "gods"— political, material, or economic, can take precedence over his commitment to God alone. In the Qur'an, faith is something people do: They share their wealth, perform works of justice, and prostrate their bodies to the ground in an ego-deflating act of prayer.

"Islam," Wikipedia

Faith everywhere
Asks for mercy
Looks for light
Begs for forgiveness
We this human breed
Want only to be loved
Honored
And eased past death
Into the promised place beyond

Is it impossible
To embrace
The faith of everyone?

Ramadan
Salaam
Dar-ah-Islam
Inshallah

In South Carolina
Scholars estimate
Thirty percent
Of the enslaved
Prayed Allahu Akbar
Inshallah
God is great
Five times every day

Once here
In the land of the free
The minarets
Mullah
Allahu Akbar
Qur'an
Ayatollah
Caliph
Dar-ah-Islam
Even the names
Were blotted out
And pushed into oblivion
And why was that?

Allahu Akbar
God is Great
Islam here was disrespected
Disconnected
Defamed
And disappeared

Sleeping under the hatred
Soon to awaken
Bearing gifts and riches
From this poor world
And the paradise beyond

Maybe the Islamic paradise
Of tropical gardens
And virgins expecting to make love
Overwhelmed
The slave-holding evangelicals

News flash:
We embrace Islam
Wherever it breathes
Wherever it bows
To Mecca
And the Ka'bah

Allahu Akbar

Inshallah

The Star-Spangled Banner

*T*HE *Star-Spangled Banner* was officially designated as the national anthem of the United States by President Herbert Hoover in 1931. The lyrics come from a poem written by 35-year-old lawyer Francis Scott Key after he witnessed the bombardment of Fort McHenry by British ships during the War of 1812. The poem was set to the tune of a popular British song, "To Anacreon in Heaven," by John Stafford Smith.

"The Star Spangled Banner," Wikipedia

> *Oh, say can you see by the dawn's early light*
> *What so proudly we hailed at the twilight's last gleaming?*
> *Whose broad stripes and bright stars thru the perilous fight*
> *O'er the ramparts we watched were so gallantly streaming?*
> *And the rocket's red glare, the bombs bursting in air*
> *Gave proof thru the night that our flag was still there*
> *Oh, say does that star-spangled banner yet wave*
> *O'er the land of the free and the home of the brave?*

FRANCIS SCOTT KEY, 1814

The twilights last gleaming
Is it gone?
Do we still await the dawn?

After too many assassinations in the night
Too many murders at noon
The guardians of death
Still muzzle us

We question
Way too much
As the good die young
And prophets disappear

The gods of war
Apparently
Have swallowed up
The Prince of Peace

The perilous fight continues
Through the night of unknowing
Battles fought endlessly
For contractors and the NRA
The rocket's red glare

Oh yes
Incredible returns on investments
The Prosperity Gospel on parade

The land of the free and the home of the brave
We say
Should not have said that
No
Should not have aired promises
Of freedom
And expectations of equality
Folks get ideas
About who they are
And who they could be

We do
We be

As elected officials
And law enforcement personnel
Sworn to protect us
Place their knees on
The necks of the crucified

And the body politic
Drowns in pandemonium

In the meantime
Notwithstanding argument and rage
Past uncertainty
Beyond misgivings
And grief
We owe the ground we stand on
And the promise of day
To patriots
Who stepped forward into the early light
And fought
For the dream of democracy

ETERNAL REST

Eternal rest grant unto them, O Lord:
and let perpetual light shine upon them.
He shall be justified in everlasting memory,
and shall not fear evil reports.

PRAYER FOR THE DEAD IN THE REQUIEM MASS

Eternal rest
Is that it?
Rest?
Like rust?
Disappearing into nothingness
I've come this far
To fall asleep and never wake?
Perpetual light shining on my bones
To what effect?
And why?

I thought light carried energy
Information
Joy

I don't want to be remembered
I want to be the one remembering
Let's not blur the obvious

The prayer:
He shall not fear evil reports
Fear evil reports from whom?
Where am I going?

Speak!

STEEPLECHASE

S TEEPLECHASE originated in 18th century Ireland when horses and riders raced from one town's church steeple to the next, the steeples used as markers due to their visibility over long distances.

Eventually, this spirited event became a worldwide equine sport. In the United States, especially in the Carolinas, steeplechase became extremely popular.

"Steeplechase (athletics)," Wikipedia

Steeplechase began
As the result of a wager
A race
What else?

Between one church steeple
And another
In County Cork

Steeds jumping streams
Soaring
Flying
Hurdling
Leaping
Vaulting
Springing
Shrubberies
Hedgerows
Dykes
and low stone walls

Spirits
Galloping
Stealing oxygen
Angel energies
Charging the air

Occasionally crashing through
Fences
And rails
Breath stopping
For sudden death

Breathe!

The Enslaved

THE TEMPLE

The local plantation house
We call it
Riverview

Corinthian columns
Fading brick
A boxwood labyrinth
Evocations of ancient Greece
The cradle of democracy

We know where we come from
We know who we are
We do

Do you?

The enslaved enjoyed it here,
Sing the descendants
Of the masters
Us
We want the best for everyone
In Carolina
At Riverview

They return relentlessly
These days
They do
To decide where they came from
They know who they are
They do

Do you?

Beautiful people
Café au lait
Some light eyed,
White teeth too
They come from the owners
And the overseers
Not to mention Africans
They know who they are

They do

Do you?

We don't know much about DNA
Establishing relationships
Memory
Like faith
Sometimes serves the soul
Better than alleles
And mitochondria

Two hundred years ago
The aristocrats who built this house
Us
Almost aristocrats
We meant well
We did
We wanted the best for everyone
We came out of no place
We created Riverview

We were kind
Measured
Considerate
We said we were
Weren't you?

Well
Yes
One little rising
Had to be crushed
Its leaders hanged on the courthouse lawn

Convicts come
With every generation
The hotheads in question
Wanted to rape the women
And massacre the men
They did

Somebody said they did

What would you have done?

Those we remembered best
Worked in the big house
Beautiful people
Some the color of wheat
Others with azure eyes

They helped us die
They helped us to be born

Wade in the water
Coming for to carry me home

We took their music
And made it our own

Yes, Ma'am

We loved one another
We still do
Don't you?

We know who we are

We do

Don't you?

Forgive, O Lord

Forgive, O Lord,
the souls of all the faithful departed
from all the chains of their sins
and by the aid to them of your grace
may they deserve to avoid the judgment of revenge,
and enjoy the blessedness of everlasting light.

FROM THE REQUIEM MASS

Once again
When do we forgive ourselves
Sometimes
Just for being alive
And ignorant
Unable to fix
The suffering of us
And anyone we choose to love

Who am I to question
Creative Source
The Light of the Universe
Who forgives the so-called souls
Of the faithful departed?

Faithful?
Did they have a choice?
Who said they sinned?
By definition
We come broken down
And dumb

Lord Jesus
You are presumably
The inner light

What grace are you supposed to give them now?
When they are already part of you
And you of them
At least in the telling?

Before the blessedness of everlasting light
And the night of unknowing
Can we not grieve?
Is there no place for tears?
Why are we torn apart
And waiting to be comforted?

Escape

South Carolina established its first slave code in 1695. The code was based on the 1684 Jamaica slave code, which in turn was based on the 1661 Barbados slave code. The South Carolina slave code was the model for other North American colonies.

The 1712 South Carolina slave code established positions of the state's racial groups:

> "Negroes and other slaves brought unto the people of this Province for that purpose, are of barbarous, wild, savage natures, and such as renders them wholly unqualified to be governed by the laws, customs, and practices of this Province."

The slave code included such provisions as:

- Slaves were forbidden to leave the owner's property unless accompanied by a white person or had permission. If a slave leaves the owner's property without permission, "every white person" is required to chastise such slaves.

- Any slave attempting to run away and leave the colony (later the state) receives the death penalty.

- Any slave who evades capture for 20 days or more is to be publicly whipped for the first offense, branded with the letter R on the right cheek for the second offense, and lose one ear if absent for 30 days for the third offense, and castrated for the fourth offense.

- Owners refusing to abide by the slave code are fined and forfeit ownership of their slaves.

- Slave homes are to be searched every two weeks for weapons or stolen goods. Punishment for violations escalates to include loss of ear, branding, and nose-slitting, and, for the fourth offense, death.

- No slave is allowed to work for pay, plant corn, peas or rice, keep hogs, cattle, or horses, own or operate a boat; buy or sell; or to wear clothes finer than 'Negro cloth.'

The South Carolina slave code was revised in 1739 with the following amendments:

- No slave is to be taught to write, to work on Sunday, or to work more than 15 hours per day in summer, and 14 hours in winter.
- Willful killing of a slave exacts a fine of £700, "passion"-killing £350.
- The fine for concealing runaway slaves is $1,000 and a prison sentence of up to one year.
- A fine of $100 and six months in prison are imposed for employing any black or slave as a clerk.
- A fine of $100 and six months in prison are imposed on anyone selling or giving alcoholic beverages to slaves.
- A fine of $100 and six months in prison are imposed for teaching a slave to read and write, and death is the penalty for circulating incendiary literature.
- Freeing a slave is forbidden, except by deed, and after 1820, permission of the legislature (Georgia required legislative approval after 1801).

"South Carolina slave codes," Wikipedia

Run
Run away fast
Run past dogs
And guns
Run straight to the dark
Through swamps
Past cottonmouths
Run north
Run west
Run past the white man
And his one drop
One drop of pain
One drop of grief
Do not stop running
Until you are
Dead
Or done
Done with the prison they call a plantation
Done with

Being told your name
Your religion
Your possibilities
Run to the light you have never seen
Only told about
Run while your legs hold out
And your heart stays strong
Run from the people who loved you
And the babies you bore
Run because you have no other choice
Run for freedom
Is that what they call it
Free
And when you are done
Then what?

You will be stronger than you ever knew
You will see horizons before you
You will know the next question
And the next direction

Maybe some day
But not now
You can look around
And see how far you've come

Maybe then

Not now

DAY OF WRATH

Dies irae, dies illa
Solvet saeclum in favilla,
Quid sum miser tunc dicturus?

This day, this day of wrath
shall consume the world in ashes,
as foretold by David and the Sibyl

FROM THE REQUIEM MASS

This day of wrath
Shall consume the world in ash

Who decided this?
Who imagined disaster on a global scale?
Why do we swallow propaganda whole?

What mind of humankind
Is so affixed on catastrophe
So drawn to death
And nothingness
That we would sing about ashes in church
Quoting the Sybil nonetheless
And David
With his psalms extolling Yahweh
The war god of the Canaanites
Forever wallowing
In bloodshed and revenge
Over enemies
Real or imagined
All in the name of God?

What trembling there will be
When the judge shall come
to weigh everything strictly!

What about the God of love?
Proclaimed the Master of Light
The Christ
Who by definition
Cannot sin

We are trapped in invincible ignorance

Who in starving
Will not steal?

Who in despair
Will not lie and cheat
To rise from hopelessness?

Who in agony
Will not choose to believe?

ANDREW JACKSON

A NDREW Jackson (1767–1845), an American soldier and statesman, served as the seventh president of the United States from 1829 to 1837, and before that, in both houses of Congress. As president, Jackson advanced the rights of the common man, as then defined. In 1835, he became the only president to completely pay off the national debt; but while he pursued reforms designed to eliminate waste and corruption, his presidency marked the beginning of the "spoils system" in American politics. Many of his actions proved divisive; historians traditionally ranked Jackson favorably among U.S. presidents, but his reputation has suffered since the 1970s, largely due to his role in the Native American removal.

"Andrew Jackson," Wikipedia

Andrew Jackson
The face on the 20-dollar bill
Politically incorrect these days

Another slaveholding
Scotch-Irish warrior
Constructing a country
Out of guns and blood

The face of White Supremacy
Evicting the indigenous
Authorizing
The removal of the Cherokee
The Chickasaw
The Seminoles
In the benighted Trail of Tears

As if the designated savages
Did not also
Rape, pillage, kidnap, slaughter, torture, kill
All of the above
Wrestling
To retain their ancestral lands

Sacred for millennia

Andrew Jackson
Fall guy
For Caucasian predators

Jackson the conquering hero
The Battle of New Orleans
The expansion west

Nobody remembers
Or cares
Two of his three adopted sons
Were Native American

He fought
For the so-called common man
And opposed the abolition
Of slavery

Life can be complicated
At its core

Complicated
Congested
Contradictory

And totally alive

Denmark Vesey

Denmark Vesey, also Telemaque (c.1767--1822) was an African American leader in Charleston, South Carolina. Born into slavery in St. Thomas, he won a lottery and purchased his freedom around the age of 32. In 1818 he was a founder of an independent African Methodist Episcopal (AME) congregation in Charleston, later known as the Emanuel African Methodist Episcopal Church after the Civil War. In June 1822, he was convicted of organizing a major slave revolt scheduled for July 14. He was executed on July 2.

"Denmark Vesey," Wikipedia

St. Thomas-born
Bermuda-bred
Denmark Vesey
Telemaque

A slave
A carpenter
A so-called insurrectionist

Labels proliferate
With Black men
Who deliberate too much

As his resume unwinds
Vesey won the lottery
Bought his freedom
And helped found Mother Emanuel
The same church where
White supremacist
Dylann Roof
Made sure
Black lives don't matter

After that
His life and execution

Is up for argument
We do know informants
Iagos all
Ruled the day with inference

After he and 35 conspirators were hanged
July 2, 1822

No historian
Has yet found evidence

No plans
No weapons

Only talk
Of freedom
Discussion of liberties
Declarations of independence

And maybe going home

Where does that leave the rest of us?

Are freedom and democracy
Still dangerous ideas?

Are silence
And surrender
And eventual execution
Still the best way
To stay alive?

Oh, Mary, Don't You Weep, Don't You Mourn

Oh, Mary, don't you weep, don't you mourn
Didn't Pharaoh's army get drowned?
Oh, Mary, don't you weep
Well, Satan got mad and he knows I'm glad
Missed that soul that he thought he had
Now, didn't Pharaoh's army get drowned?
Oh, Mary, don't you weep
Oh, Mary, don't you weep, don't you mourn
Oh, Mary, don't you weep, don't you mourn
Didn't Pharaoh's army get drowned?
Oh, Mary, don't you weep
Well, one of these nights around twelve o'clock
This old town's gonna really rock
Didn't Pharaoh's army get drowned?
Oh, Mary, don't you weep
Oh, Mary, don't you weep, don't you mourn
Oh, Mary, don't you weep, don't you mourn
Didn't Pharaoh's army get drowned?
Oh, Mary, don't you weep
Oh, Mary, don't you weep, don't you mourn
Oh, Mary, don't you weep, don't you mourn
Didn't Pharaoh's army get drowned?
Oh, Mary, don't you weep
Oh, Mary, don't you weep, don't you mourn
Oh, Mary, don't you weep, don't you mourn
Didn't Pharaoh's army get drowned?
Oh, Mary, don't you weep
Oh, Mary, don't you weep, don't you mourn
Oh, Mary, don't you weep, don't you mourn
Didn't Pharaoh's army get drowned?
Oh, Mary, don't you weep

TRADITIONAL SPIRITUAL

Oh Mary
Don't you weep
Don't you mourn
One of these nights
Around twelve o'clock
We'll go to town
And really rock

Sometimes
History overwhelms the soul
We hear constantly
Of massacres
Lynchings
Graft
Embezzlement
The list persists

Too many innocents
Subsisting
On what you can catch in the woods
Too many babies dead
Too many mommas wrecked by the wrong man

Covid
Snakebite
Rape

Oh, Mary don't you weep
Don't you mourn
One of these nights
Around twelve o'clock
We'll go to town
And really rock

Didn't Pharoah's army drown?
So did Grandma on the pond
Uncle Frank at Normandy went down
Earl got killed in Vietnam

Carla in Afghanistan
Joy Boy in a drive by
The list persists
Cut off
Gone

Who keeps saying
Pharoah's army went down and drowned?

In the meantime
We got Caesar
We got Octavian
William the Conqueror
Dracula
The Ottomans
Napoleon Bonaparte
The Raj
Hitler
Timothy McVeigh

In the meantime
As we speak
A million soldiers
Are decapitating enemies

Would that be me?

Oh Mary
Don't you weep
Don't you mourn
One of these nights
Around twelve o'clock
We'll go to town
And really rock
Civil War

King Cotton

COTTON remained a key crop in the Southern economy after slavery. Across the South, in an almost feudal system, landless farmers, Black and White, worked rented land in return for a share of the profits. Some farmers bore production costs themselves. Picking cotton was a main source of income. Rural school systems split vacations so children could work in the fields during cotton-picking.

During the mid-20th century, machines began to replace laborers. The South's rural labor force shrank during the world wars. Cotton remains a major export of the United States, with large farms in California, Arizona, and Texas.

"Cotton," Wikipedia; "King Cotton," Wikipedia

Once we eclipsed Egypt and India
Feeding textile mills
Fitting out the world

Cotton fields
Generating capital
In the antebellum South

Even as the cotton crop
Depletes the soil
Pushing planters
Further west
We argue about monuments
To war and generals

South Carolina cotton fields
Forgotten
Bare
Have become memorials
To the enslaved
Nailed to the land
Seared by sun
And overseers
Broiling

Barely breathing
Fingers bleeding
Quotas the higher power
How many bales per ten-hour day?

Come celebrate cotton
In Bishopville
The Cotton Museum
Tuesday through Saturday
Ten to four-thirty
Six dollars adults
Seniors four

WalMart
Cotton shirts
Two for ten dollars

Otherwise
Try Amazon
And look for sales

The Jaws of the Lion

Lord Jesus Christ, king of glory,
deliver the souls of all the faithful departed
from the pains of Hell
and the bottomless pit.
Deliver them from the jaws of the lion,
lest hell engulf them,
lest they be plunged into darkness;
but let the holy standard-bearer Michael
lead them into the holy light,
as once you promised to Abraham
and to his seed.

Lord, in praise we offer you
Sacrifices and prayers,
accept them on behalf of those
who we remember this day:
Lord, make them pass
from death to life,
as once you promised to Abraham
and to his seed.

FROM THE REQUIEM MASS

No doubt
We need to be delivered
From the jaws of the lion
Metaphorically
One would hope

What about the pains of Hell?
Ain't there Hell enough right here
For too many people to calculate?

We could review World War One
And Two
Auschwitz

Dachau
Bergen-Belsen
Siberia
The lynching forests of the South
Prisons for profit
The list goes on

Deliverance comes too late

Promises turn out to be but memories

We wait for rescue into light

Slavery

S OUTH Carolina asserted that the government of the United States had failed to uphold its obligations to South Carolina, specifically the refusal to enforce the Fugitive Slave Act and clauses in the U.S. Constitution protecting slavery.

While these problems had existed for a generation, the situation became intolerable due to the election of Abraham Lincoln, who was planning to emancipate the slaves. South Carolina's primary reason for its secession: increasing hostility in the non-slaveholding states to the institution of slavery.

"South Carolina Declaration of Secession," Wikipedia

Why argue
About the natural order of mankind?

Aside from I.E.D.s
(Improvised explosive devices)
Foreclosures
Unspecified viruses
We of the world
Are still swimming in slaves

Who's to say otherwise?

Even now
In the 21st century
Women and girls
Not to mention boys
They rarely do
Are bought for breeding
And other things
At bargain rates
In the global marketplace
With parents and grandparents
Counting coins

Slavery enters into us like breath
As ordinary
As birth and death
In the natural order of things

Who's to say otherwise?

Like prostitutes
Procurers
Cock fighting
People impounded
Cannon fodder
Battlefields routine
Slaughter commonplace

We are the way of the world
We buy and sell
Everything
This, an ordinary platitude

Who's to say otherwise?

We are
A social order
Hinged on hierarchy
Hard work
Profit and loss
Relentlessly

We will fight to maintain
The natural order of Man
By divine right
And obvious wisdom
We are the oligarchs
Self-appointed by our own

Who's to say otherwise?

Old MacDonald Had a Farm

Old MacDonald had a farm, E-I-E-I-O.
And on that farm he had some cows, E-I-E-I-O.
With a "moo, moo" here,
And a "moo, moo" there.
Here a "moo" there a "moo"
Everywhere a "moo, moo".
Old MacDonald had a farm, E-I-E-I-O.
Old MacDonald had a farm, E-I-E-I-O.
And on that farm he had some chickens, E-I-E-I-O.
With a "bawk, bawk" here
And a "bawk, bawk" there,
Here a "bawk", there a "bawk,"
Everywhere a "bawk, bawk,"
Old MacDonald had a farm,
E-I-E-I-O.

TRADITIONAL CHILDREN'S SONG.
LYRICS BY THOMAS D'URFEY, 1706

Old MacDonald had a farm
E-I-E-I-O.
He had pigs and goats and horses too
Anything conceivable
Making animal cries
Except llamas and cobras
Of course
Not to mention elephants

What about lions, tigers, and bears?
No aardvarks either?
Certain species don't take the heat too well

MacDonald's farm was once Indian land
The Shawnee slaughtered
The first European settlement

White men
Women and children
Gone

Before that
White men
Massacred a bunch of Cherokee
Women and children
Shamans
Et cetera
It do go on

After that, the replacement group
With bigger guns
And better ammunition
Settled in
These from Barbados
Where they had learned to handle
Slaves
And grow indigo
Rice
And cotton too

After the War of Northern Aggression
With plantations burned
And barns destroyed
Blacks went north to Baltimore
And Washington DC

We remember
When we were happy
Were we then?

Between wars
And a difficult peace

No hope of government assistance
No sign of God

We wait for agribusinesses
And timber farms
In short
The North
To buy us out

We churned butter once
And grew field peas
Okra
Corn
Picked peaches
Pickled cauliflower
Milked the cows
And waited for rain

The farm
Could be a children's paradise
Moo cows moo
Six geese a laying
Oink said the pig
Pink as bubble gum
And a partridge in a pear tree

Dreams are what we live for

E-I-E-I-O

SECESSION

Declaration of the Immediate Causes Which Induce and Justify the Secession of South Carolina from the Federal Union

> ... We, therefore, the People of South Carolina, by our delegates in Convention assembled, appealing to the Supreme Judge of the world for the rectitude of our intentions, have solemnly declared that the Union heretofore existing between this State and the other States of North America, is dissolved, and that the State of South Carolina has resumed her position among the nations of the world, as a separate and independent State; with full power to levy war, conclude peace, contract alliances, establish commerce, and to do all other acts and things which independent States may of right do.
>
> FROM THE SOUTH CAROLINA ARTICLES OF SECESSION, DECEMBER 20, 1860

Why do men
Without substantial property
Men who never owned another man
Yeomen descended from the servant class
Former convicts
And ne'er do wells
Surrender their lives
Fighting to the death
For slavery?

Do they imagine God
Will punish them
If they won't hew
To the natural order of things
The resounding euphemism
For masters and slaves?

The South in this argument
Becomes the template
For natural disaster

600,000 dead
Readjusted in 2020
Now 850,000
To include those
Dead from injuries
Fighting over the right
To buy and sell other Americans
States' rights are stronger than God
Yes, Ma'am.
Property the foundation stone
Of civilization
Ain't that so?

In hindsight
The excuses for war
Any war
Take your pick
Pick one, any one
Become pretext for slaughter
Argument for despair
And political dismemberment

All for the right to buy and sell
What we used to label
Temples of the Holy Ghost

Secession shreds
The emerging landscape
Men in waistcoats
Starched collars
Across the state
Deciding masses of yeomen
Should sacrifice their lives

We speak of slaughter
As if it were a legal brief
An op-ed opinion piece
A considered philosophy

Sure we do

We speak of rednecks too
When do we honor them?
When do we appreciate
The common man
Always uncommon
Always ready to help

P.S.
And by the way
One drop of Africa
You're blackballed from the club

Offertory

As we humbly present to you these sacrificial offerings, O Lord, we beseech your mercy, that we who did not doubt your Son to be a loving Saviour, may find in him a merciful Judge. Who lives and reigns for ever and ever. Amen.

FROM THE REQUIEM MASS

Do we blame God?
Jesus Mary and Joseph
Whoever they are
And expect them to
Open the gates of the Bastille

Let the standard bearer Michael
Lead us into holy light
All right?

Where are you Mike?
Where's Gabriel?
Ezekiel?

I'll take a cherub
If that's all you've got
Never mind the seraphim

Figures of power and light
Even sparks
Embers
Eveready batteries
Candles
Tapers
Torches
Kitchen matches

Come forth

The dead among us
Need you now

Fort Sumter

THE Battle of Fort Sumter (April 12–13, 1861) refers to the bombardment of Fort Sumter near Charleston, South Carolina by the South Carolina militia (the Confederate Army did not yet exist), the return gunfire and subsequent surrender by the United States Army. This was the battle that started the American Civil War.

"Fort Sumter," Wikipedia

April 12, 1861
Gentlemen
Why did we secede?
Were we overwhelmed
By abolitionists?

We worshipped Thor and called him Jesus
Him and his momma
Regina Mundi
Queen of the World
Didn't we Boys?
Blue-eyed deities
Their faces plastered white
Their sole intent to rule

Blacker gods were but shadows then
Specters shrouding in the night
Waiting for the centuries to come

Businessmen
Borrowers
We built domains from common soil
Rice
Cotton
Indigo

Could we not negotiate
Some settlement
For slaves?

Was it the women we feasted on?
Why war?
Why fire cannons on the government
Expecting what?

All the while
Debutantes in the Battery
Bedecked in crinoline and picture hats
Waved at bombardments
From their balconies

They

The loveliest of fantasies

Fun!

Psalm Eighteen

[1] *I love thee, O God, my strength.*
[2] *God is my rock, and my fortress, and my deliverer;*
My God, my rock, in whom I will take refuge;
My shield, and the horn of my salvation, my high tower.
[3] *I will call upon God, who is worthy to be praised:*
So shall I be saved from mine enemies.
[4] *The cords of death compassed me,*
And the floods of ungodliness made me afraid.
[5] *The cords of Sheol were round about me;*
The snares of death came upon me.
[6] *In my distress I called upon God,*
And cried unto my God:
He heard my voice out of his temple,
And my cry before him came into his ears.
[7] *Then the earth shook and trembled;*
The foundations also of the mountains quaked
And were shaken, because he was wroth.
[8] *There went up a smoke out of his nostrils,*
And fire out of his mouth devoured:
Coals were kindled by it.
[9] *He bowed the heavens also, and came down;*
And thick darkness was under his feet.
[10] *And he rode upon a cherub, and did fly;*
Yea, he soared upon the wings of the wind.
[11] *He made darkness his hiding-place, his pavilion round about him,*
Darkness of waters, thick clouds of the skies.
[12] *At the brightness before him his thick clouds passed,*
Hailstones and coals of fire.
[13] *God also thundered in the heavens,*
And the Most High uttered his voice,
Hailstones and coals of fire.
[14] *And he sent out his arrows, and scattered them;*
Yea, lightnings manifold, and discomfited them.
[15] *Then the channels of waters appeared,*
And the foundations of the world were laid bare,
At thy rebuke, O God,
At the blast of the breath of thy nostrils.
[16] *He sent from on high, he took me;*

He drew me out of many waters.
¹⁷ He delivered me from my strong enemy,
And from them that hated me; for they were too mighty for me.
¹⁸ They came upon me in the day of my calamity;
But God was my stay.
¹⁹ He brought me forth also into a large place;
He delivered me, because he delighted in me.
²⁰ God hath rewarded me according to my righteousness;
According to the cleanness of my hands hath he recompensed me.
²¹ For I have kept the ways of God,
And have not wickedly departed from my God.
²² For all his ordinances were before me,
And I put not away his statutes from me.
²³ I was also perfect with him,
And I kept myself from mine iniquity.
²⁴ Therefore hath God recompensed me according to my righteousness,
According to the cleanness of my hands in his eyesight.
²⁵ With the merciful thou wilt show thyself merciful;
With the perfect man thou wilt show thyself perfect;
²⁶ With the pure thou wilt show thyself pure;
And with the perverse thou wilt show thyself forward.
²⁷ For thou wilt save the afflicted people;
But the haughty eyes thou wilt bring down.
²⁸ For thou wilt light my lamp:
God my God will lighten my darkness.
²⁹ For by thee I run upon a troop;
And by my God do I leap over a wall.
³⁰ As for God, his way is perfect:
The word of God is tried;
He is a shield unto all them that take refuge in him.
³¹ For who is God, save God?
And who is a rock, besides our God,
³² The God that girdeth me with strength,
And maketh my way perfect?
³³ He maketh my feet like hinds' feet:
And setteth me upon my high places.
³⁴ He teacheth my hands to war;
So that mine arms do bend a bow of brass.
³⁵ Thou hast also given me the shield of thy salvation;
And thy right hand hath holden me up,
And thy gentleness hath made me great.
³⁶ Thou hast enlarged my steps under me,
And my feet have not slipped.

^{37} *I will pursue mine enemies, and overtake them;*
Neither will I turn again till they are consumed.
^{38} *I will smite them through, so that they shall not be able to rise:*
They shall fall under my feet.
^{39} *For thou hast girded me with strength unto the battle:*
Thou hast subdued under me those that rose up against me.
^{40} *Thou hast also made mine enemies turn their backs unto me,*
That I might cut off them that hate me.
^{41} *They cried, but there was none to save;*
Even unto God, but he answered them not.
^{42} *Then did I beat them small as the dust before the wind;*
I did cast them out as the mire of the streets.
^{43} *Thou hast delivered me from the strivings of the people;*
Thou hast made me the head of the nations:
A people whom I have not known shall serve me.
^{44} *As soon as they hear of me they shall obey me;*
The foreigners shall submit themselves unto me.
^{45} *The foreigners shall fade away,*
And shall come trembling out of their close places.
^{46} *God liveth; and blessed be my rock;*
And exalted be the God of my salvation,
^{47} *Even the God that executeth vengeance for me,*
And subdueth peoples under me.
^{48} *He rescueth me from mine enemies;*
Yea, thou liftest me up above them that rise up against me;
Thou deliverest me from the violent man.
^{49} *Therefore I will give thanks unto thee, O God, among the nations,*
And will sing praises unto thy name.
^{50} *Great deliverance giveth he to his king,*
And showeth lovingkindness to his anointed,
To David and to his seed, for evermore.

Someday I will know you
You are my strength
My power
My light
I like to think
Or at least imagine

In the meantime
You are only sensed
As if you hide beyond a row of hills

We call you our Rock
Our Might
Our Deliverer

By the way
Where were you at Gettysburg?
Shiloh
Fort Donelson
Chattanooga
Antietam
Yellow Tavern
Nashville
Mobile Bay
Five Forks
Gettysburg
Always that

Before the beginning
Of who we became
The Battle of Camden
Barefoot soldiers eating grass
In the glaring Carolina sun

The sorrows of death encompassed us
And pressed us down
We called upon your holy name
As boys surrendered to the dirt
Their brains blown to smithereens
Innards splattered
Dreaming dashed

Did you hurl the lightning?
Did you send the storm?

We said you saved us
Even as the majority went down.

Will you show yourself to be merciful?

We are a nation destroyed
A people in anguish
We stand convinced you will rescue us
As we lay slain and torn apart
We still believe in you
We have nothing else
Only ourselves
And we are beaten down

You breathed into us
Weapons of steel
And domination
You offered dreams of victory
Of the world we left behind
Of slaves for the taking
According to your holy laws

To please you we pursued our enemies
To please you we became invincible
Until we were dust under the feet
Of those who destroyed us

We prayed to you
To deliver us
From our enemies

Now the war is lost
The fields are burned and barren
We are reviled
And ridiculed

Still
We persist in giving thanks unto thee

And why is that?

LUX AETERNA—EVERLASTING LIGHT

Merciful Jesus, O Lord
Grant them rest
Merciful Jesus, O Lord
Grant them eternal rest.

FROM THE REQUIEM MASS,
AS ARE THE ITALICIZED PRAYERS IN THE POEM

Merciful Jesus
Who are you?

More importantly
Where are you?

Who decided
You could grant anyone rest?

We live on faith
According to the priests
And the wisdom of celebrities

Deliver me, O Lord, from eternal death
on that awful day
when the heavens and earth shall be shaken
and you shall come to judge the world by fire.

I am seized with fear and trembling
until the trial is at hand and the wrath to come:
when the heavens and earth shall be shaken.

Who will come to judge the world by fire?
Jesus, is that you?
Jesus, the Master of Love?
Shaking the heavens and the earth

Why would you do that?
I have come to understand
We will judge ourselves
That will be enough

"The wrath to come?"
What did we do?
Someone compromised our DNA
Short circuited our brains
Enveloped us in rank emotion
Made learning difficult

Yes, I am seized with fear and trembling too
Who are we?
Who are you?
Where are we going?
Speak up!
Is no one there?

These days
It seems
We have only ourselves

When Johnny Comes Marching Home Again

When Johnny comes marching home again
Hurrah! Hurrah!
We'll give him a hearty welcome then
Hurrah! Hurrah!
The men will cheer and the boys will shout
The ladies they will all turn out
And we'll all feel gay
When Johnny comes marching home.

LYRICS BY PATRICK GILMORE, 1863

War can be wonderful
When our boys come home again
Glorious in gray

Assuming they haven't seen
Too much death on the battlefield
Their best friends buried in the mud
Faces smashed to smithereens
Some men blind, some deaf
Some with souls that disappeared

None of that matters with victory
The ground strewn wide with amputated limbs
Everywhere entrails
And pandemonium

None of that matters
When you come marching home again
Hurrah! Hurrah!

Bobby
Billy
Andy J

Freddie
Jimmy
Wilson
Roy
Heroes every one

The men will cheer
And the boys will shout
Until they know
They're next to go
Commandeered into the calvary
Hurrah! Hurrah!

Charging with bayonets

The men will cheer
And the boys will shout
The ladies they will all turn out

Goddammit
Get the eyes!

Sometimes I Feel Like a Motherless Child

*S*ometimes *I Feel Like a Motherless Child*, a traditional Negro spiritual, as they were called, dates back to the slave era. An early performance of the song by the Fisk Jubilee Singers dates to the 1870s.

> *Sometimes I feel like a motherless child*
> *Sometimes I feel like a motherless child*
> *A long ways from home*
> *A long ways from home*
> *True believer*
> *A long ways from home*
> *Along ways from home*
>
> *Sometimes I feel like I'm almos' gone*
> *Sometimes I feel like I'm almos' gone*
> *Sometimes I feel like I'm almos' gone*
> *Way up in de heab'nly land*
> *Way up in de heab'nly land*
> *True believer*
> *Way up in de heab'nly land*
> *Way up in de heab'nly land*

No consolation greeting card
Or half-remembered joke
About St. Peter at the pearly gates
No rumors of ghosts
No channelers
Can bring back the dead

Psychics predicting happiness
Can soften the invading dread
Of a child abandoned
And a mother gone

"A long ways from home"
Which is what?
A house burned down?

Photographs now ash?
Stories blurred?

Anecdotes without faces
Become meaningless

Home
Apparently
Where she went
And disappeared

Singing out of tune
Off-pitch
She burned the bacon
Forgot the punch lines
Couldn't fry sunny side up
Without fracturing the yolk
Couldn't find the other shoe
The lost sock
The car keys

And sometimes
Couldn't find me

I am motherless now

And alone

A long ways

From everywhere

And almost gone

PARADISE

May the angels lead you into paradise;
at your coming may the martyrs receive you
and lead you to the holy city of Jerusalem.

May the chorus of angels receive you
and with Lazarus, once poor,
may you have eternal rest.

<small>FROM THE REQUIEM MASS</small>

May the spirits of the living and the dead
Stay with us and comfort us
As we depart this plain
Of contradiction
And paradox

Beauty and degradation
Laughter and blubbering
Discord
Occasional ecstasy
Chicken parmesan
Champagne
Making love in the afternoon
Dying on the battlefield
That's us

On this earth we have loved
Embraced
Resisted and counter attacked
Transformed where we could
And once again
Returned to our home

To sit again with the masters of light
And all those we have loved
In the presence of the Holy One

Amen

I'll Take You Home Again, Kathleen

I'll Take You Home Again, Kathleen is a popular song written by Thomas Paine Westendorf (1848–1923) in 1875. The music is loosely based on Felix Mendelssohn's Violin Concerto in E Flat Minor Opus 64 Second Movement. The song's popularity reflects many immigrants' painful loss of their countries of origin, including their friends and families back in Europe. "I'll Take You Home Again, Kathleen," Wikipedia

I'll Take You Home Again, Kathleen
Across the ocean wild and wide
To where your heart has ever been
Since first you were my Bonnie bride.
The roses all have left your cheek.
I've watched them fade away and die
Your voice is sad when e'er you speak
And tears bedim your loving eyes.
Oh! I will take you back, Kathleen
To where your heart will feel no pain
And when the fields are fresh and green
I'll take you to your home again!
I know you love me, Kathleen, dear
Your heart was ever fond and true.
I always feel when you are near
That life holds nothing dear, but you.
The smiles that once you gave to me
I scarcely ever see them now
Though many, many times I see
A dark'ning shadow on your brow.

I'll take you home again Kathleen
Across the ocean wild and wide
To where your heart has ever been

And where is home, my Bonnie bride?
Ayrshire? Antrim? The Yorkshire Moors?
Where the fields are fresh and green
And cold rain pours down
On abandoned cottages

Forsaken in famine
Where some girls go barefoot
And others go mad
Where too many babies die
And boys become fodder
For too many wonderful wars

How could I take you home again?
What fantasy entraps your heart?

Where is home, my Bonnie bride?
You speak of Mother dead and gone
The boys who loved you once
Are nowhere now
Your Daddy's disappeared at sea

You've blocked the rest
Apparently
Everything you were
Become a blur

Once you prized a scrap of lace
That reminded you of home
Another time
A mongrel
In Bishopville
Or maybe Bethune
Looked like a puppy you once knew
Buddy you thought
Or Burt

Where is home, my Bonnie bride?
Where is home, Kathleen?

We have green fields here
Sad songs to sing
And friends to cherish you

Oh! I will take you back Kathleen
To where your heart will feel no pain

Oh! If we can only find
Your home again

And I can find your heart

Peace Be with You

In the name of compassion for the earth and its people
In the name of the spirit that breathes
As you and I breathe
In the name of kindness and the creative source
Of invention, of art and technology
In the name of love
We begin and end in peace

I Confess

I confess to almighty God
and to you, my brothers and sisters,
that I have greatly sinned,
in my thoughts and in my words,
in what I have done and in what I have failed to do,
through my fault, through my fault, through my most grievous fault;
therefore I ask blessed Mary ever-Virgin, all the Angels and Saints,
and you, my brothers and sisters,
to pray for me to the Lord our God.
May almighty God have mercy on us, forgive us our sins,
and bring us to everlasting life.
Amen.

FROM MOST CHRISTIAN SERVICES IN ONE FORM OR ANOTHER

We talk about sins
Without saying what
Presumably sexual
One way to control the body politic

As bombs
And ballistic missiles
Travel silently
Across the world
Into nurseries
Hospitals
Wedding breakfasts
Blowing up babies in the name of democracy

We fixate on masturbation
And saying f . . ck

How unnecessary
Said the librarian

Telling someone to go to hell
That's unforgiveable as well

Greatly sinned against no doubt
The hierarchy
Clergy concerned
Professional holy men
And women too
Supporting politicians
Who would bury anyone in too much need
Even the need for identity

Therefore
There's a word
We ask blessed Mary ever virgin
Who thought that one up?
All the angels and saints
As defined and registered
By the Confraternity of Christian doctrine
And the Vatican office of protocol
Through my fault
Through my fault
Through my most grievous fault
Beat me
Beat me up
Drag me into depression
And self-hatred for
Holding my own

Pray for me to the Universe
May I have mercy on myself
May I forgive me my sins
Especially those that were
Guess what
Never sins at all

And at least entertain the possibility of everlasting life
Even though most of my friends don't believe
Such things are possible

I do

Amen

I Dream of Jeanie

Jeanie with the Light Brown Hair is a parlor song by Stephen Foster (1826–1864). It was published by Firth, Pond & Co. of New York in 1854. Foster wrote the song with his estranged wife Jane McDowell in mind. The lyrics allude to a permanent separation.

"Jeanie with the Light Brown Hair," Wikipedia

I dream of Jeanie with the light brown hair,
Borne, like a vapor on the summer air;
I see her playing where the bright streams play,
Happy as the daisies that dance on her way.
Many were the wild notes her merry voice would pour.
Many were the blithe birds that warbled them o'er:
Oh, I dream of Jeanie with the light brown hair,
Floating, like a vapor, on the soft summer air.

STEPHEN FOSTER, 1854

Young women
With wild hearts and merry sounds
Heal the wounds
Of war
Just by being there
Reflecting light
And song

Artless
Unaware of powers
They wield
Over ordinary folk
Like you and me
These happy sprites
Transform
The stale exchange
Of day

Beauty
Breathtaking
And innocent
Visits them for the briefest time
When they are young

Until afterwards
It too disappears
Into the dimming
And the dark

I dream of Jeanie with the light brown hair
Even now
When I am old
And quarrelsome

Anarchy arrives from everywhere
Celebrating insurrection
And announcing war

I dream of bright streams
Blithe birds warbling
And Jeanie with the light brown hair

Borne like a vapor
On the summer air

MARY BOYKIN CHESNUT

We are scattered, stunned; the remnant of heart left alive is filled with brotherly hate. Whose fault? Everybody blamed somebody else. Only the dead heroes left stiff and stark on the battlefield escape.

A DIARY FROM DIXIE, MARY BOYKIN CHESNUT, 1823–1886

In *A Diary from Dixie*
Mary Boykin Chesnut
Daughter of the Confederacy
Chronicles the agonies of war

Close your eyes
Cover your ears
600,000 dead
850,00 casualties
A nation weighted down
With mutilated flesh

Everywhere disfigurement
And death

In its beginnings
A cousins' feud
A joust
It began with flags in flight
Trumpets furious
And glad hurrahs
A pageant advancing victory

Like all good Southern wives
Who regaled
Distinguished governors
Senators
In her case generals

Mary Boykin Chesnut
Excelled
In the arts of discretion
And diplomacy

Prudent in the face of cruelty
Moderate in tone

But having eyes to see
As the scriptures go
And a heart on fire
She overrode her social code
And wrote down truths
That lived in her bones
The wrongs of slavery
The subjugation of women
And girls

And ever after
Grieved for the loss
Of her ravaged inheritance

And the slaves she once owned
And loved

She said

Once upon a time

SHERMAN'S MARCH

T HE campaign known as Sherman's March to the Sea, lasted from November
15 to December 21, 1864.

Sherman ordered his army of 62,000 men to march from Atlanta 300 miles
southeast to Savannah, Georgia and destroy everything in their path, especially
the railroads. They dynamited factories and burned down towns, farms, banks,
and courthouses. Sherman made clear his intent was to end the war. Whether the
march itself constitutes a war crime is still an intensely argued controversy. Sher-
man famously expounded, "War is Hell."

An estimated 50,000 civilians were killed during the war; possibly 1,000 dur-
ing the Savannah Campaign at the hands of soldiers pillaging. The 3rd and 4th
Amendments to the Constitution prohibit these actions.

"Sherman's March to the Sea," Wikipedia

War is hell
Declared the inferno
William Tecumseh Sherman
General
Hero
Conqueror
Rapist overseer
Priest of eventual peace

To the South
A criminal
Torching plantation houses
Munition dumps
Wrapping railroad ties around Confederates
All of the above
Depending on your birth
Bank account
And of course
What versions of history you prefer

Here in the midlands
The fire breathing energy remains
The tsunami of war
Imprinted in the sand
Plantation houses
Burned to the indifferent ground

Black folk
The underlying argument
Of everything we have come to be
Not yet part of the narrative
Yes, almost invisible then
Cheered him on

We hear them still

WERE YOU THERE WHEN THEY CRUCIFIED MY LORD?

T HE following lyrics are those printed in the 1899 *Unicorn: Old Plantation Hymns*; other variations exist.

Were you there when they crucified my Lord?
Were you there when they crucified my Lord?
O sometimes it causes me to tremble! tremble! tremble!
Were you there when they crucified my Lord?

Were you there when they nail'd him to the cross? (Were you there?)
Were you there when they nail'd him to the cross?
O sometimes it causes me to tremble! tremble! tremble!
Were you there when they nail'd him to the cross?

Were you there when they pierced him in the side? (Were you there?)
Were you there when they pierced him in the side?
O sometimes it causes me to tremble! tremble! tremble!
Were you there when they pierced him in the side?

Were you there when the sun refused to shine? (Were you there?)
Were you there when the sun refused to shine?
O sometimes it causes me to tremble! tremble! tremble!
Were you there when the sun refused to shine?

How come Southerners
Know so much about despair
And early death?

How come we know so much
About a god man on a cross
Nailed
Pierced
And crucified?

How come?

Was it Shiloh
Chattanooga

Or Gettysburg?

Where were the Edgefield Hussars?
Where was the 2nd Calvary?

What changed us
Forevermore
Unto the generations
When we understood at last
Brutality
And the compounding rage?

As history turned
The enslaved went free
They above all
Had known brutality

Those of us caught up
In war
Lay down in blood
And confusion

Yes
We were there
When they crucified my Lord
And condemned the rest of us
To sorrow
And defeat

We were there
Fighting for nobility
Honor
Pride

My God
My God
Why hast thou forsaken me?

FORGIVENESS

May almighty God have mercy on us, forgive us our sins,
and bring us to everlasting life. Amen

Somewhere
There is a presence
Deep in my soul
That speaks to me
Telling me I am forgiven
For falling off the railroad track
Crashing my car
Drowning in the surf

Metaphors intended
Allegories all

Let's get literal

Wrecking my relationships
Screaming at children
Pushing people
Who wished I were dead
Hating my own stupidity
My insistent failure at almost everything
My drama inevitably about me
The unforgiving
Insufferable me

If I am forgiven
I too must forgive
Must show mercy to the difficult
The drunks
The hopelessly bourgeois
Could be
Would-have-beens

Overfed fat-faced friends
I call my own
Feeding on gossip
And half-baked tales
Of the world and its catastrophes

Somewhere lies my soul
A presence deep
That speaks to me
Whispering

Be still

FUNERAL FOR THE WARS

Europeans frequently proclaim
You Americans never had a war
Not on your own ground
Not where it matters

You don't know reality
They imply
War being the confirmation of identity
Forgetting
Most of us came from cannon fodder
Feeding continental wars
Our ancestral generations
Delivered into conflagrations
Genealogies impounded
Identities erased
Yeomen
Peasants
Convicts
Drafted into death
Leaving wives and daughters
To be regularly raped
In the seriously civilized
European hemisphere

Here in the South
To answer the argument
We have weathered
Millennia of tribal savagery
Catawba
Mississippians
Cherokee
Sioux
Slaughtering
Dismembering

Until the Europeans came
And did the same

Discounting the depredations
Of the enslaved
Consider the American Revolution
Patriots bayonetted in the mud
And afterwards begat
Our famously uncivil Civil War
As we contemplate
More than half a million dead
Diseased
A union massacred

Hello Jim Crow
If you were black
Yellow
Brown
God help you
Brotha
Until Rosa Parks sat in the front of the bus
Dr King had a dream
And freedom rode relentlessly

Now
According to MSNBC
FOX
CNN
We wage no war on our front lawns
Harbor no fugitives
Only ourselves
Divided
Polarized
Convincing ourselves
We are one

All the while
Wondering what's next

Will we evolve
Into healers
And comforters
Or will we
Once again
Drown our fields
In blood?

We
The know-it-alls
Who never had a war

RECONSTRUCTION
The Dark Night

The Birth of a Nation

*T*HE *Birth of a Nation*, a 1915 American silent film directed by D. W. Griffith, was adapted from the novel and play, *The Clansman*, by Thomas Dixon Jr.

The film has been called the most controversial film ever made in the United States. It portrays African Americans as near-Neanderthals and sexual predators of white women; it portrays the Ku Klux Klan as a heroic force necessary to preserve the true American civilization of a white social order. *The Birth of a Nation* was the first film ever shown in the White House. It was publicly honored by the United States Supreme Court. *The Birth of a Nation* was the most financially successful film ever until *Gone with the Wind*, another film about the Lost Cause.

"The Birth of a Nation," Wikipedia

The Birth of a Nation
Came on the cusp of World War One
When colored men fought in uniform
To save democracy
According to the revisionists
Who
Unfortunately
Didn't know what they were talking about

G. Howard Tribideaux, Professor of American History, Yale University (1915)

Yes
And afterwards
They went too far
In their demands
To be created equal
Nobody's equal but us

U.S. Senator Conklin Beaumont III (1916)

The Birth of a Nation
Remains a sacrilege
Defiling the Negro with lies lodged deep within the souls of the white
overseers

The Revered Dr. Amos Jefferson, AME mother church, Lexington KY (1916)

The Birth of a Nation
Brilliantly makes the case
That the Emancipation Proclamation
Should be overturned
As soon as possible
And slaves
Once again be contained
And disciplined
Please God

Mrs. Merriweather FitzGodwin, Richmond chapter, DOC (1915)

What could be worse
Than races intermingling--
Blasphemy in the face of a Creator God?

The Rev. J. Parker Hambleton-Tillman, Jr., Chattanooga (1919)

Imagine
This story celebrating
A sacred civilization
In Charleston, South Carolina
The center of Anglo-Saxon gentility
Wonderful crinolines
And charity balls
Splendid woman
With low voices
And undeniable pedigrees
Who recite Shakespeare by candlelight
And make the most delicious lemon cakes
Not to mention music

Oh, the singing of the St. Cecilia Society!

Anonymous, Charleston SC (1918)

Charleston
The Holy City
Where in turn
Rapacious Blacks
Have recently
Caused so much
Unpleasantness
Endangering an entire economy
With brutish ignorance

Anonymous, wife of U.S. Congressman (1917)

When will reason prevail? When will the nobility of the African be held up
to the light of truth? When will we finally see democracy?

Dr. Earnest Tidewell Washington, President, The Marcus Garvey Society (1915)

Apparently
They are entitled
To rule the rest of us
Just because they used to be slaves
Arguably a step up from animals

We taught them English
Showed them how to wear shoes
And gave them Jesus Christ
What more could they ask for?

God bless and forgive Mr. Lincoln
Good thing he's dead

Superintendent, Columbia Hospital for the Insane (1915)

With *The Birth of a Nation*, the malefactors have once again forced their hideous wisdom upon us. They have once again pushed us into the dark, where to their consternation we have encountered the face of God. And once again, despite these desperate men, Jehovah praises us in the middle of evil.

Symphonia T. Singletary, from her prize-winning poetry collection,
Come Home Again (1915)

LAMB OF GOD

O Lamb of God, that takest away the sins of the world,
Grant them rest.
O Lamb of God, that takest away the sins of the world,
Grant them eternal rest.

ATTRIBUTED TO JOHN THE BAPTIST, JOHN 1:29

Lamb of God,
Who takest away the sins of the world

Do I understand the conceit
Or are we talking basic principles?

Metaphor only serves to undermine
My understanding
Of sin
Which in any case
Weighs down our spirits
Darkening our sense
Of possibility

After how many millennia
Of fighting for the good
The true
And the just
The best of us
Enlist again
For other Armageddons
To save us from the Reich
And sanctify the world

Or this time
Would it be Russia?
What about Nigeria?

Anything's possible
When it comes
To saving humankind

ALLELUIA

Alleluia
There's a word
A Hebrew expression
Praise the lord
Does he hear us?
Is he even he?

The wind hears
The sky sees
Poor us
Praising praise
Insisting on being heard

Hallelu
A variant
As we are variants
And variables
Improvisations on a theme
Of love
Tell that
To those who mourn
To brothers broken in body and mind
Halleluiah
Allelu

All things
Are known
Everything connected
Time expands
Into a universe of now and forever
Even then

As we bow low
To mystery
To light and darkness
To pain
And ecstasy
However it comes
And goes

We are awash in anonymity
Insisting on yes
Proclaiming creation

Alleluia

Allelu

The Lost Cause

Gone with the Wind (1939), the most financially successful movie in history, continued the myth of the Lost Cause—the idea that a gallant and culturally superior civilization had been destroyed by a mendacious and barbaric force coming from the North.

"Gone with the Wind (film)," Wikipedia

Scarlett O'Hara on the portico
Propped up by hoop skirts
And Corinthian capitals
Pontificating about how much she adores her slaves
Piccaninnies in particular
She appreciates ambitious gentlemen
Who will reinstate the Southern states
To their previous power and glory
For thine is the kingdom
A civilization predicated on
Decanters and demitasse
Cut crystal
Imported directly from Paris
Even Bohemia
Imagine that
Through Jesus Christ our Lord
Not forgetting silverware
Sophistication sure as second wind
Obliterating shanties
Pit latrines
Log cabins in the upstate
And convict colonies

Consider grandees with pedigrees
Venerating virgins
Surely the Caucasian kind
Revering the honor of aristocrats
And the nobility of duels

A world
Worth restoration
Even if it takes the KKK
A world of white tie de rigueur
Footmen
Sous chefs
Upstairs maids
All at the service of gentility
Good manners
In the face of drunken immigrants
Meaning Famine Irish
And pushy Jews

We did not invite the slaves
(or summon servitude)
Our forebears thought of that
They thought of everything

Nevertheless
They're here
Those Blacks belong to us
A necessary wickedness
A sin
Of course
Along with greed and rank adultery
A reality
Too terrible to contemplate
But
Emancipation can promote the cruelest letting go
You know

Better to maintain
The status quo
And work with them

And in the evenings by the fireside
Speak of Greek philosophy

Descant on Kant
Remember
Michelangelo
And mourn the death of kings
And courtesans

When civilization mattered
Courtiers bowed
Ladies curtsied
And Sacred Scripture rang

Slaves obey your masters
Said St. Paul
As Scarlett O'Hara
Knew so well

Before she died and went to Hell

P.S. Addendum

With the rest of us
Poor white folk
Wounded from the wars
Playing our bluegrass symphonies
On harp and bass and jug
Blessing the earth
And its children

We are the wild ones
The force of the future
Overriding oligarchs
And dancing in the hills

Praise life
And praise the Lord

KING OF GLORY

Lord Jesus Christ, king of glory,
deliver the souls of all the faithful departed
from the pains of Hell
and the bottomless pit.
Deliver them from the jaws of the lion,
lest hell engulf them,
lest they be plunged into darkness;
but let the holy standard-bearer Michael
lead them into the holy light,
as once you promised to Abraham
and to his seed.

FROM THE REQUIEM MASS

No doubt
We need to be delivered
From the jaws of the lion
The tiger's claws
And the crocodile

What about the pains of Hell?
Ain't there Hell enough?
Hello?

WWI and II
Auschwitz
Dachau
Bergen Belsen
Guantanamo

In the meantime
Just for the moment
I'd rather go with light

Pigging out on Rocky Road
Guinness
The occasional joint
The Super Bowl
And the relentless fantasy
Of making love

To everyone
In the neighborhood

Not Again!

Let's not talk about *Gone with the Wind*
In *A South Carolina Requiem*
For one thing
It happened in Georgia

Scarlett O'Hara
Melanie Hamilton
Rhett Butler
Ashley Wilkes

My Caucasian friends in Hollywood
Cannot understand
Why Rhett and Scarlett
Have become unacceptable

Why is Tara
Politically incorrect?

After all
Hattie McDaniel
Mammy
Her Christian name
The fat Black maid
Technically a slave
For anyone under 105
Who has not seen the film
Won the Academy Award
Best Supporting Actress 1939

Butterfly McQueen
Prissy
Another good Christian name
Also Black
Also a maid

Was by all accounts
The adorable dolt
Missing brain cells but nobody cared
I don't know nothin' bout birthin' babies
She intoned
Some people were just born to be loved

Whatever else
These girls had jobs

What's the problem here?

Why does everything
Come down to race
These days?

Minorities are jealous

Contempt their middle name

They just can't get over slavery

That must be it

LYNCHINGS

AccORDING to the Tuskegee Institute, 4,743 people were lynched between 1882 and 1968 in the United States, including 3,446 African Americans and 1,297 Whites.

The National Memorial for Peace and Justice, which opened on April 26, 2018, is the first memorial dedicated to Black people terrorized by lynching, diminished by racial segregation and Jim Crow, and overwhelmed with presumptions of guilt.

The Equal Justice Initiative (EJI), which built the memorial, investigated thousands of lynchings in the South, many undocumented. EJI was also interested in understanding the trauma the violence induced. Six million Black people fled the South as a result of the lynchings.

"Equal Justice Initiative," Wikipedia

4,743
Lynchings
The pornography of death

Terror
Invading the brain
Twisting the soul
Warping everyone involved
Hanging
Burning
Cutting
Contaminating families
Strange fruit
Putrefying on the tree

Savagery
Beyond law
Past reason
Defying God

How does one grieve for terror
Watching faces burn to ash
Castration in plain sight
Disembowelment
Blasphemy

How does one weep to see
The sons
And sometimes the daughters
Of slavery
Be hanged for speaking out
And talking back?

Sometimes
Poetry
Is the wrong approach
To violence

Dead wrong

Sometimes
Plain talk
Prose
And rhetoric
Is all the soul allows

Sometimes
Is
now

ETERNAL REST

Eternal rest give unto them, O Lord
And let perpetual light shine upon them
A hymn, O God, becometh Thee in Zion
And a vow shall be paid to thee in Jerusalem
Hear my prayer
All flesh shall come before you.

FROM THE REQUIEM MASS

Eternal rest
As if anyone not weighted down by flesh
And long experience
Even death
Would want to rest

Why rest?
Why sleep?
Why surrender into night?
Why when the dead can fly
Never again to agonize again
About being shot to smithereens
Or riddled with disease

Or losing love

All flesh shall come before you
Says the Psalm
Flesh
The mute perfection of form
Inspiring civilizations
With the beauty
Of Venuses in front of us

All this surrendered into light
They say

And who is they?
And who are we?

And who decides?

John C. Calhoun

John Caldwell Calhoun (1782–1850), was an American statesman from South Carolina who held many important positions including being the seventh Vice President of the United States from 1825 to 1832, while vigorously defending slavery and protecting the interests of the white South.

"John C. Calhoun," Wikipedia

How do you make poetry out of John C. Calhoun?
A Scotch-Irish comet blazing out of Abbeville
Thundering past sheds and barns
And cotton fields
To Yale

From the beginning
A paragon
Of uncommon brilliance
Vice President
Senator
Secretary of State
And War
Creator of armies and interstates
Notwithstanding
National intent

How does greatness
Come crashing down
Over the heads of slaves?
The South, the poor South!
His last words
No doubt referring to himself

What was he thinking?
His people came from Donegal
They understood despair
And near annihilation

He and his ilk
Ravaging Africans
Contemptuous of God
And Man

One wonders
What would have happened
If he descended from prophets
Who understood
The heart of God

Except
He was

He was

Will we ever understand
The cruelty of
extraordinary men?

Jim Crow

J IM Crow laws, state and local laws that enforced racial segregation in the
Southern United States, were enacted in the late 19th and early 20th centuries
by white Southern Democrat-dominated state legislatures to disenfranchise and
remove political and economic gains made by Blacks during Reconstruction. Jim
Crow laws were enforced until 1965.

"Jim Crow Laws," Wikipedia

Examples from South Carolina:
An 1879 statute made marriage between a white person and an Indian, Negro, mu-
latto, hybrid, or half-breed null and void. Penalty: Misdemeanor, fined a minimum
of $500, or imprisoned for not less than twelve months, or both. Ministers who per-
formed such marriages faced misdemeanor charges, subject to the same penalty.

In 1895 the State Constitution was amended to read, "Separate schools shall be pro-
vided for children of the white and colored races, and no child of either race shall
ever be permitted to attend a school for children of the other race." In addition,
Article 6 of Section 6 is rewritten to assert that each county in which a lynching
occurs may be subject to a fine of $2,000 per death. Such a measure reveals that this
type of murder is common throughout the state.

Source: Americansall.org

Note: the italicized lyrics below are from "Jump Jim Crow," Thomas D. Rice, 1828

Come listen all you gals and boys
Ise just from Tuckyhoe
I'm goin' to sing a little song
My name's Jim Crow

White men in blackface
And hoods
Hiding under the moon
Hearts weighted down
With misunderstanding
And rage
About the meaning of America

Weel about and turn about and do jis so
Eb'ry time I weel about I jump Jim Crow

We bury the ancient order
Of oligarchs and patriarchs
Druids and the damned
Darlins, it's time to go

Weel about and turn about and do jis so
Eb'ry time I weel about I jump Jim Crow

Grace envelops us
Love's unleashed
And spirits glow
These days
Hate will surely detonate
To the choruses
Of galaxies
And cloistered Carmelites
Ah so

Weel about and turn about and do jis so
Eb'ry time I weel about I jump Jim Crow

Post requiem
Past torture and death
When black becomes white
and white turns into light
When we all change places
At the rising of the moon

Weel about and turn about and do jis so
Eb'ry time I weel about I jump Jim Crow

When the night brings only tenderness
A kaleidoscope
Called Earth

Will dazzle even angels
In this universe's rebirth

Should dey get to fighting,
Perhaps de blacks will rise,
For deir wish for freedon,
Is shining in deir eyes

Weel about and turn about and do jis so
Eb'ry time I weel about I jump Jim Crow

The Mill

A t the end of the 19th century, only a few textile mills existed in the South, but by the 1920s, the South outpaced New England in yarn and cloth production. By the end of the decade, more Southerners worked in textile mills than in most other occupations. South Carolina in particular enjoyed a large population of un-skilled, non-union labor. Hours were punishing; child labor was common; workers had no workers' comp, pensions, or even decent salaries.

"Textile Industry," scencyclopedia.org

Who in the world writes poetry
Celebrating Post-Civil War
South Carolina
Textile mills
When most of us
According to the histories
Were ground down into the common dirt
Tenant farmers subsisting on grief
Blotting out memory
Trapped in overcrowded rooms
Standing at looms
The air drowning in cotton dust and chemicals
Brown lung smothering
Workers losing fingers/hands/appendages
Children trained
To turn off their imaginings
Before the boys marched off
To yet another war

They put me here when I was nine
She said
And told me to cut the threads
Ten hours a day

Before my periods
Troubles
With the boss began
Mr. Muldowney with the eyebrows
And the hands

From South Boston he said
He missed his girls

Close the door behind you
Turn the lock
Come sit on my lap
Let me look at you
You're a big girl now
We could never run the mill without you
You mean so much to me
You
Oh you
My little girl

With the prettiest blue eyes

WHITE PEOPLE

We mourn ourselves
In the night
Behind the sun

Some days
We face
The destruction of who we were
Hiroshima before our time

We have sat with the dead
These hundred fifty years
We have wept in the dark
For the boys in gray
The widows
The mothers
The children never born

We are the Lost Cause
Lost to ourselves
And our nobility

Tribal
Insular
Unto ourselves
We were founded on
Order
Hierarchy
Every person in his place
This was our DNA
Our genesis

We are now informed
Everything we are
Or have ever been
Was wrong

Be advised
We are indomitable
Resolute
Invincible
Until the end

No phone calls please
No breakfast casseroles
No lane cakes
No flowers
Definitely no carnations

And you imagined
We'd forgotten how to laugh!

THE GREAT DEPRESSION

T HE Great Depression was a severe worldwide economic depression that
took place mostly during the 1930s, beginning in the United States. It was
the longest and most widespread depression of the 20th century. It hit the South
particularly hard.

"Great Depression," Wikipedia

How you bury a Great Depression?
It lingers still
Generations bearing down
Bread lines
Suicides
Disaster awaiting the elderly
The sick
The famously infirm

How do you bury memories
Of hunger pending
Homes foreclosed
Cars on life support
Debt on overload
Poverty translated into particulars
Until at last
Despair contaminates the proud?

The cruise is cancelled
The wedding dress delayed
Abundance put away
A reckoning

What good is requiem for shame?
Says God

Where is the voice of victory?
Where is the cry of life?

Bodies lie
Unburied
In the once resplendent
Gardens of the king

The Great Depression
Now and forever
Until at last
The light breaks through
And hope returns

To the waiting fields

And the blood to come

Amnesia

I heard about smallpox yesterday
Once a seasonal plague
Without recourse or remedy

In this little Carolina town
When we complain about
Here and now
We entertain no memory
Of drinking water touched
With typhoid
And everything invisible

Women dying giving birth
Surgery forgoing anesthesia
Cancer undiagnosed
Smallpox a regular plague
Blacks forced into quarantine
In shacks
Trapped
For the duration

If they lived
Their skin destroyed
Sometimes their eyes erased

Do these particulars
Have no place in poetry?

Remember
We have all survived
In different ways
At first fighting against ourselves
And after that
At war

With the world

Have we ever known a period of peace
And perfect health
Or was that MGM in the Fifties?

Fabulous faces aglow
After two hours in makeup
When we were twenty-five
And demanded everyone be beautiful

And for a time

We were

DELIVER ME

Deliver me, O Lord, from eternal death
on that awful day
when the heavens and earth shall be shaken
and you shall come to judge the world by fire.

I am seized with fear and trembling
until the trial is at hand and the wrath to come:
when the heavens and earth shall be shaken.

FROM THE REQUIEM MASS

Who will come to judge the world by fire?
Say what?
Jesus, could that be you?
Lord, the Master of Love?
Shaking the heavens and the earth
How has it come to that?

"The wrath to come?"
What did we do?
Someone compromised our DNA
Short circuited our brains
Enveloped us in rank desire
Made learning difficult

I am seized with fear and trembling too
Who are we?
Who are you?
Where are we going?

Speak up
Cry out
Is no one there?

It seems
These days
We have only ourselves

DIXIE

I wish I was in the land of cotton, old times there are not forgotten,
Look away, look away, look away, Dixie Land.
In Dixie Land where I was born in, early on a frosty mornin',
Look away, look away, look away, Dixie Land.

Then I wish I was in Dixie, hooray! hooray!
In Dixie Land I'll take my stand to live and die in Dixie,
Away, away, away down South in Dixie,
Away, away, away down South in Dixie.

DANIEL DECATUR EMMETT, 1859

Old times there are not forgotten
Where?
In the cotton fields?
Multi-generational shame
Still beaten into the souls of the enslaved
And the formerly enslaved?

Yea, look away
Look away, Dixie Land
Look away from the whip
And the dirt
And the hanging tree

Hooray
They used to say
To live with cottonmouths
And doublewides
To suffer trash
And seduce the dispossessed

The fact is
The ancient tide has turned

The nightmare is now dream
We are the fulcrum of philosophy
Invention
And persistent wit
We are lovers bridging Black and White
And every color in between

The vision of the world to come
Is now suffused with Southern song
Blessing an unseen universe

Take your stand in Dixie
Do it
And when you die

The angels will be standing by

CAMPTOWN RACES

Camptown ladies sing dis song, Doo-dah! doo-dah!
Camptown race-track five miles long, Oh, doo-dah day!
I came down there with my hat caved in, Doo-dah! doo-dah!
I'll go back home with a pocketful of tin, Oh, doo-dah day!

Goin' to run all night!
Goin' to run all day!
I'll bet my money on the bobtail nag,
Somebody bet on the bay.

Well, the Camptown ladies sing this song doodah
Ah the Camptown racetrack's five . . .

STEPHEN FOSTER, 1826–1864

Doo-dah! Doo-dah!
Who talks like that?

Minstrel men in blackface
Impersonating
Happy slaves
Reassuring the majority
They're grateful to be here at last
Saved from predatory tigers in Nigeria
And baboons in Sierra Leone

Yes, Ma'am
Irony intended
The dark race has discovered God
He died for their sins
Praise the Lord
Doo-dah! Doo-dah!

Mr. Conductor
Pick up the pace!
And Gentlemen
Don't forget to smile!

Goin' to run all night
That's right
Away from bloodhounds
And the Klan
Not to mention the repo man
Goin' to run all day
From centuries
Nobody needed to know about
Least of all
The scholars of Timbuctoo
The engineers of Egypt
The wisdom of the mullahs
The beauty of the minarets
And the Black Madonna of Montserrat

Bet your money on the bobtail nag

Oh, Doo-dah day!

PORGY AND BESS

Porgy and Bess is an opera by American composer George Gershwin, libretto by DuBose Heyward, lyrics by Ira Gershwin.

Hall Johnson, a Black composer, in a 1936 essay in *Opportunity*, a journal published by the Urban League, wrote that Gershwin was as free to write about African Americans, then called Negroes, as any other composer could write about anything else, but he added,

> the result is not a Negro opera by Gershwin, but Gershwin's idea of what a Negro opera should be.

Decades later, James Baldwin wrote that while he liked *Porgy and Bess*, it remained a white man's vision of African American life.

"Porgy and Bess," Wikipedia

Welcome to *Porgy and Bess*
Charleston South Carolina
Depression era 1935
The Gullah community
(A nice way of saying slum)
An opera about impoverished
African Americans
In particular
A beggar
And a prostitute
In the middle of violence
Finding passion and release

Question:
What was the big attraction
For two Upper West Side
New York City-based
First Generation
Russian Americans
George and Ira Gershwin?

Were they really White men
Appropriating Black experience?

What could they possibly know
About the South
Much less African Americans
Reeling from 300 years of slavery?

Sometimes

Outsiders
Even in New York
Whose folk
Arrived from shtetls
And pogroms
The dispossessed
And the poor
Yearning to breathe free
From bigotry
And fear
Can understand
How in America
We all come
From Catfish Row
South Carolina
Circa 1935

Sometimes

We are one

Pitchfork Ben

B ENJAMIN Ryan Tillman (1846–1918) served as Governor of South Carolina from 1890 to 1894, and as a United States Senator from 1895 until his death in 1918. A white supremacist who opposed civil rights for Black Americans, he defended lynching on the floor of the U.S. Senate, and frequently ridiculed Black Americans in his speeches. Ironically, his younger brother, George Tillman, spoke out against the one-drop rule in the South Carolina Legislature, arguing that most likely every man there had at least a drop of Black blood. The younger Tillman prevailed, but the horrors of Reconstruction continued for another several generations.

"Benjamin Tillman," Wikipedia

Pitchfork Ben Tillman
One drop
And you're done
Condemned
Cursed
Boy, get off the sidewalk
Pick up your booty
And disappear

Is this what we've come from?

What does it take
To dislodge society
And break up
Ancient injunctions
In the face of
Furious preservationists

What new Jesus
Can resist
Pitchfork Ben?
What power within us
Lingers that we do not know?

Despite what you've been told
Put away the wisdom of the overseers
Ignore the shibboleths of greed
Observe the eagle carefully

And decide if you can fly

Holy, Holy, Holy

Holy, holy, holy
Lord God of hosts!
Heaven and earth are full of your glory.
Hosanna in the highest!

FROM THE REQUIEM MASS

Holy, holy, holy
Lord God of hosts![

What are hosts?
Do we know?

Our prayers are filled with questions.
Are not questions holy in themselves?

Heaven and earth are full of your glory
Where is heaven then?
Over the rainbow
Or deep inside our fragile hearts?

Is Heaven a place?
A state of mind?
An attitude?
Or special effects at MGM?

Hosanna
There's another word
Never used
Except at Mass
And probably in Israel
Two thousand years ago

Heaven and earth

Earth we know about
About Heaven

We wonder

ALL PERSONS BORN

A MENDMENT XIV from the United States Constitution
SECTION 1.

*All persons born or naturalized in the United States, and subject to
the jurisdiction thereof, are citizens of the United States and of the
state wherein they reside. No state shall make or enforce any law
which shall abridge the privileges or immunities of citizens of the
United States; nor shall any state deprive any person of life, liberty,
or property, without due process of law; nor deny to any person
within its jurisdiction the equal protection of the laws.*

All persons born
Naturalized
Or otherwise assembled
Packaged
And duly marketed
On sale or not
In these United
Are altogether equal

Not to mention
Guess again
Citizens
Of Planet Earth
We
The native-born
Bedraggled
Beaten down
Get out of my way
Post Neanderthal
Human race
Are altogether equal too

Which means what
In terms of armies
Languages
Bank accounts
And various political philosophies?

We are enfranchised
Emancipated
And practically congealed
One to another

Deprive one
You deny the rest of us

We are not to be abridged
Our voice condensed
Or liberty withheld
Without expected hurricanes

One day
We will be free to roam the world
Without border guards
Papers
Passports
And customs checks

One day
We will be unimpeded
Footloose
Free

This is our planet

And the promise of home

LIFT UP YOUR HEARTS

Lift up your hearts.
We lift them up to the Lord.
Let us give thanks to the Lord our God. It is right and just.
It is truly
that we should give you thanks and praise, O God, almighty Father,
for all you do in this world,
through our Lord Jesus Christ.
For though the human race
is divided by dissension and discord, yet we know that by testing us
you change our hearts
to prepare them for reconciliation.
Even more, by your Spirit you move human hearts that enemies may speak
to each other again, adversaries may join hands,
and peoples seek to meet together.
By the working of your power
it comes about, O Lord,
that hatred is overcome by love,
revenge gives way to forgiveness,
and discord is changed to mutual respect.
Therefore, as we give you ceaseless thanks with the choirs of heaven,
we cry out to your majesty on earth,
and without end we acclaim:

FROM THE REQUIEM MASS

Holy, Holy, Holy Lord God of hosts.
Heaven and earth are full of your glory.
Hosanna in the highest.
Blessed is he who comes in the name of the Lord.

The Catholics say
Sanctus
The Evangelicals
Employ the everyday vernacular

Holy
Holy
Holy Lord

A good starting point
At least for questioning

Heaven and Earth
Are full of your glory

Earth
Sky
And sea
Are also chockablock with grief
Kalashnikovs and HIV
Genocide and glioblastoma
Oh yes
Not to mention
You and me

How does the glory of our DNA
The majesty of Michelangelo
Bach
Billie Holliday
And Satchmo
How about the Internet
Grant peace to the mother
Of the dying child?

Bless is he who comes in the name of the Lord
We sometimes say
Who he?
Jesus comes and goes
In the telling
He rides on a donkey
Towards Jerusalem
And death

Afterwards
We keep hearing
He died for our sins

And opened the gates of Heaven itself

If you say so

He might say it differently

15th Amendment

Section 1

The right of citizens of the United States to vote shall not be denied or abridged by the United States or by any State on account of race, color, or previous condition of servitude.

What
Hardcore supremacists
In February 1870
Decided Black folk
In point of fact
Were not allowed to vote?

It's not like educated gentlemen
Had yet been able to figure out
How to bomb
Nagasaki and Hiroshima
Or construct
A Dachau
Bergen Belsen
Auschwitz One
And Two
Or Birkenau

In the meantime
The body politic
Clearly needed underlings
To serve drinks on the veranda

Yes Sir
Stepin fetchit
Boy
And make them ask
For permission
To breathe

As for women
Any woman
Once again
Define your terms
Black
White
Or polka dot
They just weren't there yet

At least Black men had a leg up
On the White girl
Sorry
Misplaced metaphor

Except those Blacks
Who had not yet memorized the Gettysburg Address
And maybe the Constitution
A reasonable request for
Any so-called upstart
Deciding to vote

Evolution
Comes dropping slow
Apparently

In the meantime
The Holy Spirit remains
On oxygen

The Great Migration (1916–1970)

AFTER World War I, when race relations in South Carolina had seemed to be improving, many returning African American servicemen were met with race riots and violence. Job opportunities once again became scarce. For these reasons, in the years between the wars, at least a million Black people immigrated to the northern cities in what was called The Great Migration.

"Great Migration (African American)," Wikipedia

Towards the end of World War One
Fifty years past Emancipation
Reconstruction
And institutional mendacities
Otherwise known as lies

Millions of Black folk
In the middle of the night
In the quicksand called Dixie
Packed up their clothes
In cardboard suitcases
And paper bags
Climbed into the broken-down family Ford
Drove north
And never looked back

At the start of the Civil War
57% of South Carolina
Was African American
At that time known by other names
Now it's 27.3%
What happened?
Gosh!

They had suffered enough insanity
At the hands of fundamentalists
Who worshipped
A well-known
Caucasian deity

By and large
So-called
Caucasians hadn't a clue

How about me?

How about you?

Are you Caucasian too?

CIVIL RIGHTS

John Lewis

J OHN Robert Lewis (1940–2020) was an American statesman and civil rights activist who served in the United States House of Representatives for Georgia's 5th congressional district from 1987 until his death in 2020.

> *Our actions entrench the power of the light on this planet. Every positive thought we pass between us makes room for more light. And if we do more than think, then our actions clear the path for even more light. That is why forgiveness and compassion must become more important principles in public life. Anchor the eternity of love in your own soul and embed this planet with goodness. Lean toward the whispers of your own heart, discover the universal truth, and follow its dictates.*
>
> *Release the need to hate, to harbor division, and the enticement of revenge. Release all bitterness. Hold only love, only peace in your heart, knowing that the battle of good to overcome evil is already won. Choose confrontation wisely, but when it is your time, don't be afraid to stand up, speak up, and speak out against injustice.*

JOHN LEWIS,
ACROSS THAT BRIDGE: LIFE LESSONS AND A VISION FOR CHANGE

(2012, public library)

He called forgiveness
And compassion
Light

He used the term
The eternity of love

Discharge the need to hate
He said
Release the enticement
Of revenge
As if anyone would hear

What would be sweeter than delivering
The Klan into fire?

Let go of bitterness
Release
He said again

Really?

Bitterness can be wonderful
When you've been swallowing fire
And drowning in hurricanes
Of tears

John Lewis
Where do you find your strength?
Where do you discover light?

Stop speaking in platitudes
Tell us the truth
About evil in our time

When your skull was crushed
By barbarians
Did it let in light?
Is that how it happened?

Will we need to have our
Heads be fractured too
For us to understand?
For us to see?

John Lewis
The ambassador of light

4,743

How can we leave lynchings to one poem?
Do we get off on thunder
Exploding in our brains
Dragons devouring our hearts
As our Black Yeshua
Is stripped
Eviscerated
Castrated
Hanged
And burned to soot?

We brought him here
Dragooned him
We and our ancestral ghosts
One and the same
Specters in the blood
Investing authority
In us
Their progeny

Constrained
Controlled
Overworked

We ravished him
Her
Whoever
Raped
Regardless of gender
Regardless of soul

He was our shadow

The ritual by the tree
Builds one breath at a time
Like theatre
And intercourse

And death

ORANGEBURG MASSACRE

THE Orangeburg Massacre refers to South Carolina Highway Patrol officers in Orangeburg, South Carolina shooting approximately 200 protestors on the South Carolina State University campus on February 8, 1968. Three African-American men were killed and 28 other protesters were injured.

"Orangeburg massacre," Wikipedia

Who remembers Orangeburg
Another dried-up
Out-of-date agrarian depot
Railway yard?

Some say
All it needs are slaves again
To get it up and running
Yassuh
That
And the second coming
Of he who said
I have not come to bring peace
But a sword

1968
The year of dime-a-dozen deaths
Bobby Kennedy
Martin Luther King
Kent State coming fast

In Vietnam
Oh that
895 South Carolinians dead
What about the Vietnamese?
That too

We say racism
And slavery
Were the engines of assassination

What about war?

Once again
Follow the money

Who profited?
Who called peacemakers
Communists?
Anything to keep the war machine in gear

Black men die
When they resist
Protest
Scream against inequity
Otherwise
They are left to twist
In the incendiary sun

Regarding Orangeburg
Massacres are all the same
Why cavil about particulars?
Even the dead look identical
Twisting in their graves
Surrounding spirits
Blowing wild

The working class wants
Bread without circuses
The relentless argument

Once again
Caucasian cops
Attempting to contain a hurricane
Black radicals arguing for equality

Musicians whose music
Holds thunderstorms
And the rhythm of the tides

Orangeburg
3 dead
28 wounded
Another day in the Midlands

We move on
We have no choice

I Have a Dream

O N August 28, 1963, the Rev. Martin Luther King, Jr. delivered his powerful *I Have a Dream* speech at the Lincoln Memorial in Washington, DC. He challenged the nation to hold to its creed that all men are created equal. He said he dreamed that one day the children of slaves and slaveowners would sit together as brothers, and that one day children would be judged not by their skin color but by what he called the content of their characters.

"I Have a Dream," Wikipedia

Martin
Your dream marks us forever
Assaulting us in the night
Subverting our sleep
With freedom
Justice
Brotherhood
Digging into our souls
Demanding definition
And accountability
Words whispering we are one

Do we yet not understand
Why
All men are created equal
Written before all Americans could vote
And women too
White
Black
And in-between
Still wondering
Why their truths were not yet evident

Martin
Tell us your dream again
You say your eyes have seen the glory

Of the coming of the Lord
You say you've been to the mountain top
And you've seen the Promised Land.
You say you're not fearing any man

We're not there yet
Martin
We're not there

Martin
Tell us your dream

Tell us again

MISS EARTHA KITT

E ARTHA Kitt (born Eartha Mae Keith (1927—2008), was an African-American performer/activist with an international following, especially known her 1953 recordings of "C'est si bon" and the Christmas song, "Santa Baby." Orson Welles called her the "most exciting woman in the world." In 1968, her career in the U.S. detonated after she made anti-Vietnam War statements at a White House luncheon. Ten years later, she made a successful return to Broadway.

"Eartha Kitt," Wikipedia

Miss Eartha Kitt
International chanteuse
Up from North
South Carolina
Next to St. Matthews
Santa Baby
Hey!
Who was her father?
Who was ours?
Black and White
Mixing
Churning
The all-American way
With just a touch
Of the Continent
C'est si bon
Exploding at the White House lunch
Offending those sweet dear ladies
Who entertained the opinion
About American boys
Black and White
Dying for freedom
In Vietnam
Except you said
No
It was corporate greed

That's not too smart
Miss Kitt

You raised
The specter of race
You and Dr. King
My God

You lifted your voice to First Lady
Lady Bird
That won't work
Remember
She planted daffodils along the Mall
Sweetpea
Marigolds
How downright wonderful

You're expected to get in line
Miss Eartha Kitt
Learn to be polite
Genteel
Considerate
You must have been socialized
That way
In North
South Carolina
No?

Remember where you came from
After all
They remember you

We do

Thank God for you
Miss Eartha Kitt

Thank God for you

The Kaddish

Magnified and sanctified is the great name of God throughout the world, which was created according to Divine will. May the rule of peace be established speedily in our time, unto us and unto the entire household of Israel. And let us say: Amen.

May God's great name be praised throughout all eternity. Glorified and celebrated, lauded and praised, acclaimed and honored, extolled and exalted ever be the name of thy Holy One, far beyond all song and psalm, beyond all hymns of glory which mortals can offer. And let us say: Amen.

May there be abundant peace from heaven, with life's goodness for us and for all thy people Israel. And let us say: Amen.

May the One who brings peace to the universe bring peace to us and to all the people Israel. And let us say: Amen.

"Kaddish," Wikipedia

Give thanks to the Jews
Celebrate the people of the book
Do not bow low to an idol in the sky

The children of Israel
Have made us understand
We need not be worshipping the sun
The moon
The gods in the forest
And the sea

However obvious in the telling
Yahweh came to earth

A warrior deity
Drenched in the blood of enemies

After Abraham
Listen up
Theology, so called
Continued to evolve

His chosen people --
They chose themselves
Should not everyone choose themselves?
Have through the succeeding centuries
Brought justice to earth
Compassion to strangers
Light to the shadows
And beauty to the night

Jews are the givers
That is their covenant
Between I Am Who Am
And the world of flesh
And mud
And the human heart

They have given us prophets
Scholars
And seers
To lead us from the lands
Of darkness
And blood
Into a place of questioning

The life of the mind

L'Chaim!

Postscript: Some things
Override history

And the works of Man
Even in the proud plantations
Along the rivers of the South

Some things
The wisdom of Yahweh
Even at his worst
Standing outside of history
And judging it for what it is

Injustice
Division
And rage

Among Southerners who said they believed
And had no clue
No suspicion
About the heart of God

Nearer, My God, to Thee

Nearer, my God, to Thee, nearer to Thee!
E'en though it be a cross that raiseth me,
Still all my song shall be, nearer, my God, to Thee.

Nearer, my God, to Thee, nearer to Thee!
Though like the wanderer, the sun gone down,
Darkness be over me, my rest a stone;
Yet in my dreams I'd be nearer, my God, to Thee.
There let the way appear, steps unto Heav'n;
All that Thou sendest me, in mercy giv'n;
Angels to beckon me nearer, my God, to Thee.
Then, with my waking thoughts bright with Thy praise,
Out of my stony griefs Bethel I'll raise;
So by my woes to be nearer, my God, to Thee.
Or, if on joyful wing cleaving the sky,
Sun, moon, and stars forgot, upward I'll fly,
Still all my song shall be, nearer, my God, to Thee.
There in my Father's home, safe and at rest,
There in my Savior's love, perfectly blest;
Age after age to be nearer, my God, to Thee.

LYRICS BY SARAH ADAMS;
MUSIC BY LOWELL MASON, 19TH CENTURY

I've often wondered
If I tumble off a cruise ship
Into the Arctic sea
And slip below an iceberg
Frozen stiff
Will someone come and rescue me?

Souls were never meant
To linger at the bottom of the sea

Wouldn't you agree?

Theologians speculate that
God
Otherwise known as Thee
Sometimes Thou
Sometimes Wow
Is everywhere
Omnipresent

But the ocean can be freezing cold
Too demanding even for divinity
Too difficult for rescuing

Even me

Maybe in the end
When all is said and done
And undone
That's what dreams are for

And why we invented fun

LAZARUS

A READING from the Holy Gospel according to John, 11:1–57
The story of Lazarus exemplifies the Christian belief in life beyond death;
this belief marks the American South as a culture of deep faith in the midst of
suffering and death.

*1 Now a certain man was sick, Lazarus of Bethany, of the village of Mary
and her sister Martha.*

*2 And it was that Mary who anointed the Lord with ointment, and wiped
his feet with her hair, whose brother Lazarus was sick.*

*3 The sisters therefore sent unto him, saying, Lord, behold, he whom thou
lovest is sick.*

*4 But when Jesus heard it, he said, This sickness is not unto death, but for
the glory of God, that the Son of God may be glorified thereby.*

5 Now Jesus loved Martha, and her sister, and Lazarus.

*6 When therefore he heard that he was sick, he abode at that time two days
in the place where he was.*

7 Then after this he saith to the disciples, Let us go into Judaea again.

*8 The disciples say unto him, Rabbi, the Jews were but now seeking to stone
thee; and goest thou thither again?*

*9 Jesus answered, Are there not twelve hours in the day? If a man walk in
the day, he stumbleth not, because he seeth the light of this world.*

*10 But if a man walk in the night, he stumbleth, because the light is not in
him.*

*11 These things spake he: and after this he saith unto them, Our friend
Lazarus is fallen asleep; but I go, that I may awake him out of sleep.*

*12 The disciples therefore said unto him, Lord, if he is fallen asleep, he will
recover.*

*13 Now Jesus had spoken of his death: but they thought that he spake of
taking rest in sleep.*

14 Then Jesus therefore said unto them plainly, Lazarus is dead.

*15 And I am glad for your sakes that I was not there, to the intent ye may
believe; nevertheless let us go unto him.*

*16 Thomas therefore, who is called Didymus, said unto his fellow-disciples,
Let us also go, that we may die with him.*

*17 So when Jesus came, he found that he had been in the tomb four days
already.*

18 Now Bethany was nigh unto Jerusalem, about fifteen furlongs off;

19 and many of the Jews had come to Martha and Mary, to console them concerning their brother.

20 Martha therefore, when she heard that Jesus was coming, went and met him: but Mary still sat in the house.

21 Martha therefore said unto Jesus, Lord, if thou hadst been here, my brother had not died.

22 And even now I know that, whatsoever thou shalt ask of God, God will give thee.

23 Jesus saith unto her, Thy brother shall rise again.

24 Martha saith unto him, I know that he shall rise again in the resurrection at the last day.

25 Jesus said unto her, I am the resurrection, and the life: he that believeth on me, though he die, yet shall he live;

26 and whosoever liveth and believeth on me shall never die. Believest thou this?

27 She saith unto him, Yea, Lord: I have believed that thou art the Christ, the Son of God, [even] he that cometh into the world.

28 And when she had said this, she went away, and called Mary her sister secretly, saying, The Teacher is her, and calleth thee.

29 And she, when she heard it, arose quickly, and went unto him.

30 (Now Jesus was not yet come into the village, but was still in the place where Martha met him.)

31 The Jews then who were with her in the house, and were consoling her, when they saw Mary, that she rose up quickly and went out, followed her, supposing that she was going unto the tomb to weep there.

32 Mary therefore, when she came where Jesus was, and saw him, fell down at his feet, saying unto him, Lord, if thou hadst been here, my brother had not died.

33 When Jesus therefore saw her weeping, and the Jews [also] weeping who came with her, he groaned in the spirit, and was troubled,

34 and said, Where have ye laid him? They say unto him, Lord, come and see.

35 Jesus wept.

36 The Jews therefore said, Behold how he loved him!

37 But some of them said, Could not this man, who opened the eyes of him that was blind, have caused that this man also should not die?

38 Jesus therefore again groaning in himself cometh to the tomb. Now it was a cave, and a stone lay against it.

39 Jesus saith, Take ye away the stone. Martha, the sister of him that was dead, saith unto him, Lord, by this time the body decayeth; for he hath been [dead] four days.

40 Jesus saith unto her, Said I not unto thee, that, if thou believedst, thou shouldest see the glory of God?

41So they took away the stone. And Jesus lifted up his eyes, and said, Father, I thank thee that thou heardest me.

42And I knew that thou hearest me always: but because of the multitude that standeth around I said it, that they may believe that thou didst send me.

43 And when he had thus spoken, he cried with a loud voice, Lazarus, come forth.

44 He that was dead came forth, bound hand and foot with grave-clothes; and his face was bound about with a napkin. Jesus saith unto them, Loose him, and let him go.

45 Many therefore of the Jews, who came to Mary and beheld that which he did, believed on him.

46 But some of them went away to the Pharisees, and told them the things which Jesus had done.

47 The chief priests therefore and the Pharisees gathered a council, and said, What do we? for this man doeth many signs.

48 If we let him thus alone, all men will believe on him: and the Romans will come and take away both our place and our nation.

49 But a certain one of them, Caiaphas, being high priest that year, said unto them, Ye know nothing at all,

50 nor do ye take account that it is expedient for you that one man should die for the people, and that the whole nation perish not.

51 Now this he said not of himself: but, being high priest that year, he prophesied that Jesus should die for the nation;

52 and not for the nation only, but that he might also gather together into one the children of God that are scattered abroad.

53 So from that day forth they took counsel that they might put him to death.

54 Jesus therefore walked no more openly among the Jews, but departed thence into the country near to the wilderness, into a city called Ephraim; and there he tarried with the disciples.

55 Now the passover of the Jews was at hand: and many went up to Jerusalem out of the country before the passover, to purify themselves.

56 They sought therefore for Jesus, and spake one with another, as they stood in the temple, What think ye? That he will not come to the feast?

57 Now the chief priests and the Pharisees had given commandment, that, if any man knew where he was, he should show it, that they might take him.

I am the resurrection and the life
He that believeth in me,
Though he were dead
Yet shall he live

Believest thou this?

Seriously?

Definitely in the category
Of "we shall see"

Believe in me
Or else
You're going down
To the gravel pit

In the meantime
It seems reasonable to assume
If we were meant to live forever
That will happen nonetheless
Whether we believe in Jesus
Mohammed
Confucius
Princess Summerfallwinterspring
Ayawasca
Or the Academy Awards

In the meantime
Yes
Can't we have fun
With an Israeli carpenter's
Pronouncements
On the meaning of life?

Especially when he comes across
Like Osiris
And Mario the Magician

Combined

That

And a compassionate God

THE LAST SUPPER

On the day before he was to suffer, on the night of the Last Supper,
He takes the bread and gave it to his disciples, saying: Take this, all of you,
and eat of it,
for this is my body, which will be given up for you. Matthew 26:28.

The poetry is complete
In the eating of flesh
Preternatural cannibals
We
Devouring the body of the god

Where do we go from here?
The drinking of the blood?
Will we be stronger then?
More compassionate?
When will we raise the dead?

The body on the lynching tree
The castrated
Mutilated dead

The bodies at Shiloh
And Chambersburg
Antietam
And Ypres
Verdun
Iwo Jima
It all runs together
The ancestral memory of who we are
Black and White
Dismembered
Red
A river of adjectives
Shamed

Despoiled
Names conveying grief
That does not end

This is my Body
Take ye and eat

Says who?

In Memory of Me

In a similar way, when supper was ended, he took the chalice, gave the chalice to his disciples, saying: Take this, all of you, and drink from it, for this is the chalice of my blood, the blood of the new and eternal covenant, which will be poured out for you and for many for the forgiveness of sins. Do this in memory of me. Matthew 26:28

The chalice of my blood
Of the new and eternal covenant
Drink from it, he says
In memory of me

Who could forget you?
You are famous for your death

For the forgiveness of sins
Night and day
In a million churches
And cathedrals
Father forgive them
They know not what they do
Except they do
The murderer knows his prey
The monster his meat
The devil his due

Does anyone understand
Transubstantiation?
Do you?
The wine is now blood
Consecrated
For the forgiveness of sins
And too many crimes to remember

What am I wanting?
I am now and forever an open wound
In the middle of meadows
And making love

In the meantime
Deliver us from evil

It's come to that

Amen

THE LORD'S PRAYER

Our Father who art in Heaven
Hallowed be thy name
Thy kingdom come
They will be done
On earth as it is in Heaven.
Give us this day our daily bread
And forgive us our trespasses
As we forgive those who trespass against us
And lead us not into temptation
But deliver us from evil
Amen

You shine within us
Outside us
Even darkness shines
When we remember
Utters the ancient Aramaic

The question is
How did we forget?

How can we see
The shining light
When we are overcome
By night?

Open your ears to the cries of children
And your heart to the suffering within
Where you will begin to know
Why you are here

Now and forever

In the meantime
Deliver us from evil

Christ Almighty
As my surgeon father used to say
Remembering his day

Amen

Baptists

B APTISTS form a major branch of Evangelical Christianity. They account for more than a third of all Protestants. South Carolina is 20 percent Baptist. No other Protestant denomination comes close in size.

"Baptists," Wikipedia

What to say about Baptists
The Holy People of the South
The best of them lighted from within
Their birthright sanctity
In spite of themselves?

Even the worst of them
As people go
Come to us
Unfailingly kind

Well, they do
Even if they cuss
Even if they sometimes
Own the cocktail hour

Why pretend otherwise?
They're people too
Aren't you?

If in the greater and the lesser
Scheme of things
The Bible is revealed
To be not revealed
Only invented
By poets
Copied by monks
And sanctioned by authorities
Southern Baptists have decided otherwise

So there

Black Baptists
Do better with praise
They've figured out the power of love
They had no other choice

In the meantime
They sing
Like nobody's business

Whites can sing too
You know
Sometimes
Sort of
Maybe
So they say
You just don't hear
Five thousand years of Africa
The calls of our beginnings
The cries of humankind
In their manufactured sound

My Baptist acquaintances
In New York and Hollywood
Complain about their church
As if it stifled them

The fact is, it never did
It only opened their hearts
And souls

How terrible is that?

MOTHER OF GOD

Hail Mary full of grace
The Lord is with thee
Blessed art thou among women
And blessed is the fruit of thy womb
Jesus
Holy Mary Mother of God
Pray for us sinners
Now and at the hour of our death
Amen

FROM AN ANCIENT PRAYER ADDRESSING MARY,
THE MOTHER OF JESUS

Holy Mary
Mother of God
Is that you?

How about Isis?
Aphrodite anyone?
Are they not mothers of gods
And possible goddesses
Fountains of infinite wisdom too?

The caring of a mother's love
Is that you?
Just you
With numerous masks and assorted names
Hiding out from village atheists
And professional skeptics with
Sledgehammers
Blow torches
Wrecking machines
Who tell us you are but a fantasy?

Lo
We know who you are
Comforting us
As we die
Dissolving
Into the infinite dark

Do we fade away
Into nothingness?
How could that be
When you speak to us daily
Whispering
Through centuries enveloped by the night?

The hour of our death
Comes presently
Our lives before us in a flash

We come
We go

Mother of God
Whoever you are
Be there
You hear?

Now
And at the hour of our death

Amen

GLORY BE

Glory be to the Father
And to the Son
And to the Holy Ghost
As it was in the beginning
Is now
And ever shall be
Amen

TRADITIONAL PRAYER

Scientists say
We entertain a trillion stars
In our tiny galaxy
And beyond us
Lie a trillion other galaxies
Each with a trillion other stars

Some say
Some
Hardly scientists
We were seeded by the Pleiades
As the Pleiades themselves
Were seeded by a parent star
A billion years ago
Or so

Still others will tell you
Time as we know it
Is never linear
It's now
Everything is now
In different
Overlapping
Intersecting

Energies

Is now
And ever shall be

Where does that leave me
Looking to fix lunch?
Does my overlapping energy
Sustain me
Or must I look in the cupboard
For canned tuna fish
Maybe mustard
Bread
Milk
And mayonnaise

Material things
An assemblage of atoms
Mostly water
Mixed in with air
Somehow in a linear universe.

What does this have to do
With glory be
To the Father
And to the Son
And to the Holy Ghost

Seems more like glory be
To here and now
To tuna fish
Salt and pepper
A slice of pickle
Maybe mustard
And mayonnaise

From one generation to the next

Is now
And ever shall be

God bless us all

Amen

WE SHALL OVERCOME

*W*E *Shall Overcome* is a gospel song which became a protest song and an anthem of the American civil rights movement. The song is commonly understood to be descended from *I'll Overcome Some Day*, a hymn by Charles Albert Tindley published in 1901.

"We Shall Overcome," Wikipedia

We Shall Overcome
We shall overcome
We shall overcome someday.
Oh, deep in my heart, I do believe,
We shall overcome someday.

The song says
We shall overcome
Someday

Except
We have already overcome
Some day was yesterday

After sorrow
And blood
After jubilation
And hope that rose with the morning sun
We understand at last
All times are now

We put a name
Around everyone
Encompassing
The dark and the light
The deaths
The births
The destruction of bodies

And the power of light
The murder of the innocents
And the rising tide of joy

Our power comes
With the force of hurricanes
And the majesty of storms
We contain the earth and sky

Yes
We have overcome
We are the world

Our names are written
In letters of gold
Within the heart of God

Amen

New Beginnings

America the Beautiful

O beautiful for spacious skies,
For amber waves of grain,
For purple mountain majesties
Above the fruited plain!
America! America!
God shed His grace on thee
And crowned thy good with brotherhood
From sea to shining sea!

LYRICS BY KATHARINE LEE BATES, 1859–1929

We begin with spacious skies
And amber waves of grain
Heading inescapably
To God
Shedding grace
And crowning good
With brotherhood
And dreams

We are a people of promise
Not yet realized
We are a perfection only dreamed about
Of beauty in the telling
Of assured equality
And grace under fire

We have come
From pogroms
And famine
We have been cannon fodder
In too many wars to count
We are the issue of rape
And religious overkill

We are the children of serfs
Indentured servants
And aristocrats gone mad

We have arrived
Illiterate
And bold

Coming
To quotas
And closed doors
Labeled
Shamed
Our offspring
Blamed for the sins
Of the establishment
i.e. annihilating Indians
And enabling slavery

With us
All the while
Dreaming in the dark
Of ourselves created equal
Endowed by our Creator
With certain unalienable rights

After generations
Upon generations
Of our children trapped in the textile mills
Our men in the mines
Our mothers bent over in the fields

We are told to be grateful
We got away from dirt
Dust bowls
And foreclosures
Assuming we ever owned the land
No, good Christ

The land owned us

From sea to shining sea
They say

Trouble is
I've never seen the sea
My dad did once at Normandy

One thing's for sure
I'll never be hungry again

As God is my witness
I have guns
And ammunition now
And more importantly

I have me

A Mighty Fortress Is Our God

A mighty fortress is our God, a bulwark never failing;
Our helper He, amid the flood of mortal ills prevailing:
For still our ancient foe doth seek to work us woe;
His craft and power are great, and, armed with cruel hate,
On earth is not his equal.
Did we in our own strength confide, our striving would be losing,
Were not the right Man on our side, the Man of God's own choosing:
Dost ask who that may be? Christ Jesus, it is He;
Lord Sabaoth, His Name, from age to age the same,
And He must win the battle.
And though this world, with devils filled, should threaten to undo us,
We will not fear, for God hath willed His truth to triumph through us;
The Prince of Darkness grim, we tremble not for him;
His rage we can endure, for lo, his doom is sure,
One little word shall fell him.
That word above all earthly pow'rs, no thanks to them, abideth;
The Spirit and the gifts are ours through Him Who with us sideth;
Let goods and kindred go, this mortal life also;
The body they may kill: God's truth abideth still,
His kingdom is forever.

MARTIN LUTHER, 1529; TR. FREDERICK HEDGE, 1853

Christ Jesus
Master of Love
Prince of peace
When did you become a warrior?
What madness in our humankind
Brought you into war?

We cannot live without enemies
It seems
Ancient foes
The Prince of Darkness
Devils in our midst

Who created this lexicon?

From one age to the next
We live and die for Jesus
Yahweh
Mohammed
Ganesh
How about Buddha?
Osiris anyone?

Turn the other cheek
He said
Presumably after we've stabbed
Garroted
Slashed
Impaled
Our enemies

What good does it do if you only love those who love you back?
He said again
And once again

Who needs schmaltz?
Sounds good on Sunday
Monday, let's put it away
Our survival cries for blood

To the Department of Defense
You are Thor
You are Jupiter
Our strength
Our guardian deity
You are
The God who lives
Through Jesus Christ our Lord
Our bulwark
And our warrior

Vietnam

T HE Vietnam War, officially fought between North Vietnam and South Vietnam, was a conflict in Vietnam, Laos, and Cambodia from November 1, 1955 to the fall of Saigon on April 30, 1975. North Vietnam was supported by the Soviet Union, China, and other communist allies. South Vietnam was supported by the United States, South Korea, the Philippines, Australia, Thailand, and other anti-communist allies. Estimates of the number of Vietnamese soldiers and civilians killed range from 966,000 to 3 million. Some 275,000–310,000 Cambodians, 20,000–62,000 Laotians, and 58,220 U.S. service members also died in the conflict; a further 1,626 remain missing in action.

"Vietnam War," Wikipedia

The battles of blood and bone
Were gone
Babies were being born again
Girls had not forgotten how to laugh
MGM resuscitated musicals
We had Woodstock afterwards
And free love in the fields

Thank you
Jesus
You rescued us through unrelenting nights
Of revolutions
Civil War
Reconstruction
World Wars One and Two
For what?

To be delivered into Vietnam?

Officially anti-Communist
Vietnam
Yet another crusade for
The bottom line

Big Business
And corporate intent
Contractors fighting for freedom
And the Dow

How does one make poetry
To celebrate insanity?

How does one applaud
The surrender of saints?
The best of America
Boys and girls
Sacrificing
Their bodies and their souls
For freedom
And manifest destiny

How could they have known
The corruption of barbarians?

Wade in the Water

Wade in the water
Wade in the water, Children
Wade in the water
God's gonna trouble the water
Who's that young girl dressed in red
Wade in the water
Must be the children that Moses led
God's gonna trouble the water

Wade in the water, Children
Wade in the water,
God's gonna trouble the water
Who's that young girl dressed in white
Wade in the water
Must be the children of the Israelite
Oh, God's gonna trouble the water
Wade in the water, wade in the water, Children
Wade in the water,
God's gonna trouble the water
Who's that young girl dressed in blue
Wade in the water
Must be the children that's coming through,
God's gonna trouble the water, yeah

TRADITIONAL SPIRITUAL

Wade in the water
Children
Wear your red and white
Don't forget your blue
Wear your baseball caps
Carry the kitty carefully
She's about due

Bring the Carolina coon dog
Pit bull

Retriever mix
Bring two

Hold hands in the water
Children
Stay close
Be safe
Make sure you do
Splish-splash
I was takin' a bath
Make noise in the water
Children
Be sure to sing along
How about Hip hop
Rap a tap
American songbook
Rock 'n roll
So God can't miss you
Children

And the angels
Will venture forth

CHERAW

J OHN Birks "Dizzy" Gillespie (1917–1993) was an American jazz trumpeter, bandleader, composer, educator, and singer of international renown. If you visit Cheraw, South Carolina, his statue stands in the middle of town.

"Dizzy Gillespie," Wikipedia

Dizzy Gillespie
Ain't you somethin'
Bud um
Bum
Bebop
Bum
Sittin' there
In the middle of Cheraw
Pee Dee
That complicated every little sound
Ba dooie
Wha
Put the cotton pickin' place
On international radar
Ya waaa
We heard
We heard
Pee Dee
Cheraw
Jazz don't predict the downbeat
It jus' comes
Overlapping
Underpinning
Unexpected
Middle of nowhere
Ya da
Zah

Complexity
Innovation
Multi-layered
Planetary jazz
John Birks Gillespie
1917–1993
Jazz trumpeter
Angel song

In the beginning
Was the word
Ba do
Ba daba
Do

And the word
Was with God

Wa do
Badooie
Wha

And so, Sir

Were you

The Sufis

As more and more Muslims move into South Carolina, we consider the Sufis. Sufism is the mystical arm of Islam. Mainline Islam, like most organized religions, largely emphasizes practical expressions and behaviors, whereas Sufism celebrates the interior life.

In the Islamic mystical tradition, the reality of "I" is not separate from the Ultimate Reality. Ibn al Arabi, the 12th century Islamic mystic from Andalusia, writes, "The eyes with which we look back at God are the same eyes with which God looks at us."

"Sufism," Wikipedia

What is this precious love and laughter
Budding in our hearts?
It is the glorious sound
Of a soul waking up!

HAFIZ (C. 1320–1389)

Once again
We remind ourselves
Thousands of Muslims
Maybe Sunni
Sufi anyone?
Hardly Presbyterians
Notably not Seventh Day Adventists
Or Carmelite nuns
Arrived with the Africans enslaved
And continue to come today

Nothing we know can disappear
Not cry
Not song
Not the sound of wind and wave

As spirit lingers
In the breath
We too
White
Black
Whatever we are
Inherit
Invisible imams
And minarets
Praising the presence of God

Allah
You are always here

In Charleston
Aiken
Spartanburg
Daufuskie
Columbia
Greenville
And unincorporated municipalities
Throughout the state

Been here since the beginning

Ali Akbar
Inshallah

SUNSET LODGE

An internationally known brothel, the Sunset Lodge, founded in 1936, was a white frame house on U.S. Highway 17 three miles south of Georgetown. The clientele included college students, millionaires, and members of the Boston Red Sox baseball team, en route to spring training in Florida. State legislators were frequent visitors. The owner Hazel Weiss, born Bennett, insisted on standards of dress and behavior. In 1969, Sheriff Woodrow Carter closed the lodge, which had been protected by officers and granted anonymity by the press.

"Sunset Lodge," scencyclopedia.org

Ordinary white frame house
Don't forget the neon sign
U.S. Highway 17
What else?

Oh, that

Women unfolding
In the heat
Of so-called clientele
Students
Seamen
Millionaires
The Red Sox baseball team
Legislators
Bankers
Probably priests
Undoubtedly white men
Escaping their girlfriends
And wives

Putting aside
Emotions
Intimacy
And the women they married till

Death do us part

Sheriff Carter closed Sunset Lodge in '69
That's one account
More to the point
A well-dressed gentleman
The color of cinnamon
Maybe mahogany
Showed up
Looking for comfort and
If you'll pardon the expression
Cooze

In that split second
Wham bam Thank you Ma'am
No questions asked
The Lodge shut down

Where is the comfort now?

Where is the advertised
Self-proclaimed
Unconditional
Love for men
Hoes are famous for?

Times, they are a-changin'

And will change again

Lust springs eternal
Except when it's shut down

Notwithstanding
Contradictions
Complications
And apologies

We shall overcome
One day

Yes, Ma'am

MARY MAGDALEN

Seeking me, you sank down wearily,
you saved me by enduring the cross,
such travail must not be in vain.

Righteous judge of vengeance,
award the gift of forgiveness
before the day of reckoning.

I groan as one guilty,
my face blushes with guilt;
spare the suppliant, O God.

Thou who didn't absolve Mary Magdalen
and hear the prayer of the thief
hast given me hope, too.

My prayers are not worthy,
but Thou, O good one, show mercy,
lest I burn in everlasting fire

FROM THE DIES IRAE (DAY OF WRATH) IN THE REQUIEM MASS.
THE ITALICIZED VERSES BELOW ARE ALSO FROM THE DIES IRAE.

All this originally in Latin no doubt
Otherwise
English
Even Swahili
Or Portuguese
Who would believe it?

Who would sing
About the Magdalen
Religiously reviled
By theologians without a clue
Mixing all the Marys

Good or bad
Deliberately conflating identities?

Woman
As Mystery, right?
Humanity comes last

A piece of ass
Ten cents a dance
Two-dollar whore
A mystical groupie
So sorry for her sins

Give me a place among the sheep,
and separate me from the goats,
placing me on Thy right hand.

When the damned are confounded
and consigned to keen flames,
call me with the blessed.

All this, in minor key
And the keening of flames
Was it really that bad?
That horrible?

I pray, suppliant and kneeling,
a heart as contrite as ashes;
take Thou my ending into Thy care.

That day is one of weeping,
on which shall rise again from the ashes
the guilty man, to be judged.

Therefore spare this one, O God,
merciful Lord Jesus:
Give them rest. Amen.

Yes

And give me rest as well. Amen

White Privilege

I thought I was Irish
Scottish
Scotch
Something like that
Not exactly upper crust
We came with freckles
And eviction notices

Grandfather raised in a cattle shed
No plumbing
Heat
Penicillin
Or for that matter
History

We were the Negroes of Europe they said
Descent from Norman overlords
And Gaelic chiefs
Made no difference now
Irish Catholics
Branded at birth
Scots Scotch Irish almost worse
Crude people dontcha know?
Shame our inheritance
Our overweening tribal pride
Proof of mediocrity

These days
Identity's turned on a dime
We've risen from the demographic dead
We're white
No, we're white supremacy
Got that?

My cousin Sean's best friend
Tyrone Jefferson
Special Forces
West Point graduate
Georgetown master's in foreign policy
Café au lait
Gets stopped by the police
Six or seven times a year

In the meantime
He's scheduled for another tour
He can't say where

These days
My people overpopulate the private clubs
Crowd the White House
Infiltrate the Social Register
What's left of it
Occupy the Stock Exchange
The Pentagon
Goldman Sachs
As once again
We bomb Afghanistan

Over pre-prandials
We talk about times
When we were oppressed
And marginalized
No Irish
Need apply
No Irish and dogs
Before we took revenge
Before we were white
Whiter than ice
Supremacists

And sometimes we invite Tyrone
That would be Captain Jefferson

To listen in and be amazed
To learn the history
Of true blue
American
Aristocrat
Barbarians

Slainte everyone

The Creed

I believe in one God, the Father almighty, maker of heaven and earth,
of all things visible and invisible.
I believe in one Lord Jesus Christ, the Only Begotten Son of God,
born of the Father before all ages. God from God, Light from Light,
true God from true God, begotten, not made, consubstantial with the Fa-
ther; through him all things were made.
For us men and for our salvation he came down from heaven,
and by the Holy Spirit was incarnate of the Virgin Mary,
and became man.
For our sake he was crucified under Pontius Pilate, he suffered death
and was buried, and rose again on the third day in accordance with the
Scriptures.
He ascended into heaven and is seated at the right hand of the Father. He
will come again in glory to judge the living and the dead
and his kingdom will have no end.
I believe in the Holy Spirit, the Lord, the giver of life, who proceeds from
the Father and the Son, who with the Father and the Son is adored and
glorified, who has spoken through the prophets.

THE CREED: A MEMORY OF A HUNDRED RITUALS AND FRAGMENTS OF
PRAYERS COMING DOWN THROUGH THE GENERATIONS

These days
What to believe?

Do you believe in life?
Is that too easy?
What about love?
Sounds like a greeting card

The Father Almighty?
Which means what?

Here we go again
The Father God

The war-god of the Canaanites
Besieging humanity for the past five thousand years
Our side and their side
With little regard
For the god within
Or is that too simple a conceit?
Too simple
And too obscure?

And in Jesus Christ his only son our Lord
Fourth Century revelation
Father Son and Holy Ghost
Same thing as a shamrock
No?

Three in one
Triplets apparently
Your move

Mon dieu
Where does sacrilege begin?
Or is blasphemy a word
Used only by librarians
When
Insanity would better serve?

Jesus the Master of Love
The bringer of wisdom
These days transformed by authoritarians
Into an icon
A loyalty oath
God love him
That simple man from Nazareth

After which he ascended into heaven
And sits at the right hand of the Father
Come to judge the living and the dead

Is that how we handle
A thousand million light years
Of stars
And galaxies?

No doubt
Another religious war
About to boom

Amen

BUDDHISTS

As Asians move into South Carolina, many bring with them their Buddhist beliefs. So too, many home-grown Americans have come to embrace this ancient tradition believed to have originated in India sometime between the 6th and 4th centuries BC.

"Buddhism," Wikipedia

Buddhists have led me to believe
That when I die
I will become a speck of light
Floating in eternal night
The phenomenon
Some call a soul
Adrift

If that's death
I'd rather disappear
And be done with it

Earth has become my anchor
Gaia my ground
Humanity
My reference point
Eros my home

Who wants to float?

No wonder
We reincarnate
And come back quick
To Carnivale
And Broadway babies
To yachts in the harbor
To Haagen Dazs
And rum

Such a deal

Anything but
Sisters of the Holy Atmosphere
And
Spirit hovering
Detached
And done

Dylann Roof

D YLANN Storm Roof (born April 3, 1994) is an American white supremacist
and mass murderer convicted of killing nine people, all African Americans,
on June 17, 2015 during a Bible study class at Emanuel African Methodist Episcopal
Church in Charleston, SC.

"Dylann Roof," Wikipedia

Mother Emmanuel
African Methodist Episcopal Church
110 Calhoun Street
Charleston 29401
Founded 1816
Welcomes you
To our discussion group
Little white boy
Wandering son
21
Come here
Let us talk about blessings

At first sight
This sweet child looked lost
Lost to history
Justice
Reckoning
Cast adrift
Mislaid
Misplaced
Mostly
From himself

Were there red flags
And warning signs?
Did thunder crash
And blackbirds caw?

Black churches
Welcome everyone
We do
We are everyone too

What wounds from
Four hundred wars
Of plagues
Pandemics
Foreclosures
Broken down machinery
Insults from the country club
And credit denied?

What suffering persisted
In the poor boy's mind
Socialized now
And then
And when
To blame minorities
For everything

Dylann Roof
Four Star general
of White Heritage

You murdered nine of us
Why was that?
We forgave you
Why was that?

Black churches
Welcome everyone
We do

We are everyone too

Abide with Me

Abide with me; fast falls the eventide;
the darkness deepens; Lord, with me abide.
When other helpers fail and comforts flee,
Help of the helpless, O abide with me.

Swift to its close ebbs out life's little day;
earth's joys grow dim; its glories pass away;
change and decay in all around I see;
O thou who changest not, abide with me.

I need thy presence every passing hour.
What but thy grace can foil the tempter's power?
Who, like thyself, my guide and stay can be?
Through cloud and sunshine, Lord, abide with me.

I fear no foe, with thee at hand to bless;
ills have no weight, and tears no bitterness.
Where is death's sting? Where, grave, thy victory?
I triumph still, if thou abide with me.

Hold thou thy cross before my closing eyes;
shine through the gloom and point me to the skies.
Heaven's morning breaks, and earth's vain shadows flee;
in life, in death, O Lord, abide with me.

Lyrics by Henry F. Lyte, 1793–1847

I have heard tales
Of friends and relatives
Careening into death
With glee and jubilation
Crying
"It's all true!"
Apparently referring to the light
And love
Awaiting on the other side

Why then the gloom
Why the crucifix
Why religion
Why creed
Why the eternal labyrinth of mind?

What have they seen?

Figures of light
At the end of a tunnel
Eerie in the description?

We are taught to hope
To believe
Rather than to know
To transcend our minds
As if direct experience
Of another world
Could not be possible

Not here

They should be reaching out to us
The spirits
The gods

If they are truly love
Let them embrace us first
And we will abide with them

PRESIDENT OBAMA

O N June 18, 2015, President Barack Obama delivered an address after the massacre of the nine African Americans at the Emanuel AME church bible study group by a White Supremacist they invited to join their group:

"Barack Obama," Wikipedia

. . . Any death of this sort is a tragedy. Any shooting involving multiple victims is a tragedy. There is something particularly heartbreaking about the death happening in a place in which we seek solace and we seek peace, in a place of worship.

Mother Emanuel is, in fact, more than a church. This is a place of worship that was founded by African Americans seeking liberty. This is a church that was burned to the ground because its worshipers worked to end slavery. When there were laws banning all-black church gatherings, they conducted services in secret. When there was a nonviolent movement to bring our country closer in line with our highest ideals, some of our brightest leaders spoke and led marches from this church's steps. This is a sacred place in the history of Charleston and in the history of America.

At some point, we as a country will have to reckon with the fact that this type of mass violence does not happen in other advanced countries. It doesn't happen in other places with this kind of frequency. And it is in our power to do something about it. I say that recognizing the politics in this town foreclose a lot of those avenues right now. But it would be wrong for us not to acknowledge it. And at some point it's going to be important for the American people to come to grips with it, and for us to be able to shift how we think about the issue of gun violence collectively.

The fact that this took place in a black church obviously also raises questions about a dark part of our history. This is not the first time that black churches have been attacked. And we know that hatred across races and faiths pose a particular threat to our democracy and our ideals.

The good news is I am confident that the outpouring of unity and strength and fellowship and love across Charleston today, from all races, from all faiths, from all places of worship indicates the degree to which those old vestiges of hatred can be overcome. That, certainly, was Dr. King's hope just over 50 years ago, after four little girls were killed in a bombing in a black church in Birmingham, Alabama.

He said they lived meaningful lives, and they died nobly. "They say to each of us," Dr. King said, "black and white alike, that we must substitute courage for caution. They say to us that we must be concerned not merely with [about] who murdered them, but about the system, the way of life, the philosophy which produced the murderers. Their death says to us that we must work passionately and unrelentingly for the realization of the American Dream."

And when we have finished
Considerations of strategy
And talk of history
And collective guilt
Will we have the wherewithal
To grieve?

How do we do that?
And when?

We grow silent in the face of death
We walk a line
Or try to
We work at normalcy
Until we erupt without warning
And completely lose control
The worst of it
Convulsions
Nightmares
Screams

As onlookers tell us it's all right
To cry
Appropriate to feel

The fact is
Nothing's appropriate
In the face of death

We are surrounded
By ghosts of the millions
Who perished on the slave ships
Died in the hold
Served up into the deep
And by the six hundred thousand
Who were slaughtered in plain sight
In our fabulous civil war
Still alive
Still surrounding us

The Charleston Nine
Unbeknownst to commentators
Who look for meaning
In despair
Are still here
On site
Still breathing
Still investigating Holy Writ

They have nowhere else to go

At least
Not anytime soon

Drugs

MORE than 93,000 Americans died from drug overdoses in 2020, including illicit drugs and prescription opioids—a 2-fold increase in a decade. Source: CDC

Opioid overdose deaths in South Carolina increased proportionately through 2013. Since then, the rate has increased from 5.2 deaths per 100,000 persons to 13.1 deaths per 100,000 persons in 2016—equivalent to 247 and 628 deaths. From 2013 to 2016, deaths related to synthetic opioids (mainly fentanyl) and heroin-related deaths rose from 50 to 237 deaths, and from 32 to 115 deaths, respectively.

In 2015, 4,490,916 opioid prescriptions were filled in South Carolina—about 109 opioid prescriptions per 100 persons compared to the national opioid prescribing rate of 70 opioid prescriptions per 100 persons (IMS Health).

South Carolina has the 9th highest rate of new HIV infections in the country. But the most alarming discovery is how young these patients are—some as young as 13 to 19 years. In fact, according to the CDC, in South Carolina for young adults between 20 and 24, 55 out of every 100,000 are infected with HIV every year, one of the highest rates in the country.

"Centers for Disease Control and Prevention," Wikipedia

Statistics carry their own truths
Why pontificate
About the Blood of the Lamb
The glory of Israel
The Communion of Saints
When death arrives en masse?

The wonders of science
And technology
History
And possibility
Working together
Mean little to people in pain

Why here
The cradle of the Confederacy
Home of too many questions to count
Too many people descended from those beaten down
The enslaved
And the indentured whites
Souls overwhelmed
With oligarchs
And self-proclaimed aristocrats

Their message:
You are born subordinate

With that
Comes alcohol
Opioids
Fentanyl
Nectars of the gods
And ultimate release

Once addicted
We will forsake this place
Wandering
And begin to die
Dreaming of gardens
And wonderful gods
Touching us
Telling us we are loved
From all eternity

Oh
That the waking world
And the self-proclaimed aristocrats
Could wander with us
And dream

Of better times to come

Nobody Knows the Trouble I've Seen

Nobody knows the trouble I've seen
Nobody knows my sorrow
Yes, nobody knows the trouble I've seen
But glory, Hallelujah
Sometimes I'm standing crying
Tears running down my face
I cry to the Lord, have mercy
Help me run this all race
Oh Lord, I have so many trials
So many pains and woes
I'm asking for faith and comfort
Lord, help me to carry this load
Nobody knows the trouble I've seen
Well, no, nobody knows but Jesus
No nobody knows, oh the trouble, the trouble I've seen
I'm singing glory, glory Hallelujah
No nobody knows, oh the trouble, the trouble I've seen
Lord, no nobody knows my sorrow
No nobody knows, you know the trouble
The trouble I've seen
I'm singing glory, glory, glory, Hallelujah!

TRADITIONAL SPIRITUAL

Nobody knows the trouble I've seen
Nobody knows my sorrow
Nobody knows
Except
My poor analyst
The long and the short:
Confusion reigns

She says
Says it plain
Don't you go runnin' to no Lord
You got to come to terms

With you
Y'hear?
Jesus has enough to do
Dealin' with psychopaths
Schizophrenics
White supremacists
Pole dancers
And death bed conversions

Who is me?
I say

Did you say
Woe is me?
She says

I said no
I said
Who is me?
Who?

I don't even talk right
Don't think right
Don't deal right

Don't

Don't what?
She says

Jesus knows
I say

She says forget him

I say
I can't forget
Nobody

Not him
Not nobody
Jesus stands next to me
He knows
He sees
He seed
He bleed for me

Religious fanatic
She says
Closing her notes
Handing me a bill

Here's your receipt

Yes, Ma'am

Yes, Sir

There's nothing more
I can do for you
Goodbye

Nobody knows the trouble I've seen
Nobody knows but Jesus

In which case
Jesus?
Jesus?
Where you be?

Are you really standing next to me?

THESE DAYS

The Christ! Ah, that is an abyss of light. We must be careful lest we fall into it.

ATTRIBUTED TO FRANZ KAFKA

"Franz Kafka," Wikipedia

These days
We are the biggest army
The world has ever known
Our military bases encircling
The known and unknown world
Saving us from insurgents
And spies

These days
We come to terms
With Jesus meek and mild
No longer
A plaster statue in pastels
An androgynous castrato
Cradling a lamb

These days
We are clever
We worship Thor
And call him Jesus
No distinction required
And no apologies

Pastors pray on the battlefield
To the Lion of Judah
Red faced with rage and resolution
While we're worshipping

Yahweh
The God of Gods
And then some
Demanding the Universe
Crush our enemies
Real or imagined

These days
We have little time for piety
And its restraints
No patience
For platitudes
That belong on greeting cards

These days

OLD WHITE MEN

Donald Trump, President
William Barr, AG
Mitch McConnell, Senate Majority
Custodians of the Republic
Names forgotten
As fast as they evaporate

Old white men
The present bugaboo
Explaining everything
Gone off the rails

Once again
Why are we wrangling
Left and right
Black and White
Male Female
North South
Cat Dog
Name calling
Polarized
Vituperation
Shit

Back to the argument
Old white men
What about Einstein
Verdi
Sondheim
Freud
How about Marx?
How about Michelangelo?

Are they old white men too?
Am I?
What's your label?
What's your brand?

Two hundred years ago
Or so
When slavery was king
The face of God
Was White
Or was supposed to be

The rest of the human race
Ninety-nine point nine percent
Was in the telling
Dumb
Dark
Dirty
Alliteration for the desperate

Edison
Benz
Alexander Graham Bell
Olmsted
Fleming
Henry Ford
Old white men
Again

Let's list their sins
And omissions

Let's get the
Anti-Catholic
Anti-Semitic
Racist
Misogynist
XY chromosomes

Out of the way

Don't forget
Secessionists
Oligarchs
Slave holding misogynists

And their subservient
Wives
And mistresses

Old white men
The cause of our suffering
The reason for our despair

Everyone take a breath

Feel better now?

Good

Get over it

Reprise: The Star-Spangled Banner

Oh, say can you see by the dawn's early light
What so proudly we hailed at the twilight's last gleaming?
Whose broad stripes and bright stars through the perilous fight,
O'er the ramparts we watched were so gallantly streaming?
And the rocket's red glare, the bombs bursting in air,
Gave proof through the night that our flag was still there.
Oh, say does that star-spangled banner yet wave
O'er the land of the free and the home of the brave?

Francis Scott Key, 1814

Oh, say
Can you see freedom
Or is it born invisible
Like God?

Bright stars gleam through dawn
Reminding us
We are conceived in light

With bombs bursting in air
We were always there
Always brave
Forever proud
Or were we?
Did we have to struggle
To understand equality?

Oh, say
Can you see those
Jazz possessed
Hip-hop blessed
Love confessed
Star-spangled warriors

Look again

Have you guessed?

Yes, Baby
That would be us

THE DIG

T OPPER, an archaeological site along the Savannah River in Allendale County, is noted as a location of artifacts which some archaeologists believe indicate human habitation earlier than the Clovis culture, previously believed to be the first people in North America.

"Topper site," Wikipedia

Down near Walterboro
There's a dig
Not yet advertised
With three
Count 'em strata
Of what we call Native American now
They had other names for themselves
Mississippians
Muskogee
Catawba
Pee Dee
Chicora
Edisto
Santee
Yamassee

A dig
Beyond dating
Some archeologists speculate
Fifty thousand years

You've seen one sherd
You've seen 'em all
Says Alfred E. Neuman
Resident archeologist
And public intellectual
Arguing the human race
Has always depended on vases and bowls

To be sure
Skeletons and severed heads
Sacrificial victims
To one god or another
Show up everywhere

Where are these people now?
What did they teach us?
What did they know?

They too engaged in tribal wars
Slaughtering enemies
Marking boundaries

They too made love
Plucked goldenrod
Trillium
Bloodroot
Pale gentium
Butterfly weed
And presumably
Told stories
Sang sad songs
And wondered who they were

In time
Earthquakes and ice
And otherwise
High-ranking deities
Erased monuments
And memory
Destroying art
Obliterating history

Why do we need to know
From whence we have come
When we are certain

We have been born in blood
From one generation to the next?

We build
We fight
We destroy the best of us

Were Mississippians
And Muscogee

Any better

Any worse?

Deliver Us from Evil

But deliver us from evil

FROM THE LORD'S PRAYER

After Holocausts
Pogroms
Plagues
Occasional Hiroshimas
The rapes of Nanking
And ordinary massacres
Who are we
But rank survivors
Culled like animals
Mere accidents
Statistically improbable

We are the children of famine
And war
Canaries in the coal mines
Cannon fodder
Descending down
From anonymity

We say to you
Deliver us
As if you ever did

Why would you now?
Look at us
Destroyed by:
Pick one of the above
Not to mention one of the below:
State terrorism

Medical experiments
Torture
"I can't breathe"

How brave we have been
To be human
How heroic
To rise up from sleep
And begin again
To remind ourselves to love

Deliver us
O God
From an unconvincing universe

If you cannot show yourself

Deliver us from you

Go Tell It on the Mountain

Go tell it on the mountain
Over the hills and everywhere
Go tell it on the mountain
Our Jesus Christ is born
When I was a seeker
I sought both night and day
I asked the Lord to help me
And he showed me the way
Go tell it on the mountain
Over the hills and everywhere
Go tell it on the mountain
Our Jesus Christ is born

TRADITIONAL SPIRITUAL

Go tell it on the mountain
And maybe social media
What about Facebook
Twitter
And Instagram?

Go tell it on the mountain
Jesus Christ is born

You'd be advised
To shout it out
On NBC
CBS
Network
Cable
Even over the telephone

Cry economic justice
Universal health care
A guaranteed minimum wage

But whatever you do
Don't make the connection
Between Jesus Christ
And justice for all
Religion 'sposed to be
About Heaven
Not here

Don't talk about Christ and war
Christ and capital punishment

When children go hungry
Keep government out
Democracy's 'sposed to be
About Individuality

Go tell it on the mountain
Until the heart aches
And the stomach rots
From fear and habitual despair
Wondering how many thousand years
We got
Until we rise again
And light shines bright
In every human heart

Go tell it on the mountain

The time is now

For Thine Is the Kingdom

For thine is the kingdom
The power
And the glory
Now and forever
Amen

FROM THE LORD'S PRAYER

The power and the glory
Means what?

Let us speak plainly now
Why must our idea of God
Be identified with our worst ambitions
And the overriding tyranny of man?

We have been bludgeoned
With the glory of emperors
Armies of the republic
And the threat of nuclear bombs

How do we hear the whispering of God?
Telling us we are loved
When we are deafened by the name droppings
Of miscreants
And the destroyers of worlds

We have been the barbarian tribe
Thrashing before thrones
Genuflecting to self-appointed royalty
And worshipping wealth

Is this the song
Of the carpenter from Nazareth
Who disappeared in blood
Leaving behind
A dream that does not die?

AMERICA

F IRST performed in public on July 4, 1831, at a children's Independence Day
celebration at Park Street Church in Boston. The first publication of *America*
was in 1832.

"America (My Country 'Tis of Thee)," Wikipedia

My country, 'tis of thee,
Sweet land of liberty,
Of thee I sing;
Land where my fathers died,
Land of the pilgrims' pride,
From ev'ry mountainside
Let freedom ring!

SAMUEL FRANCIS SMITH 1808–1895

Originally
God save the king
That's appropriate

Sweet land of liberty
At least for bankers
Landlords
And historians

Land where my fathers died
Actually mine died
In every miserable war
On Planet Earth
Seven Years War
Thirty Years War
War to End All Wars
Cannon fodder for empire
God save the Tsar
The Califate

The armies of Chiang Kai Shek
The Ottomans
Gallipoli
Ypres
Where does it end?

God Save the Second Amendment
The right to bear arms
Land of the Pilgrim's Pride
If you were a Pilgrim
Good for you
God save the witches
Baptists
Catholics
Jews

Let freedom ring!
Ring dem bells
Beat the drum
Evolve into hot jazz
And Mardi Gras
Kwanza
Seder
Ramadan
And Requiem Mass

Along with sweet land
Let's have some hot sauce
Shrimp n grits
Ratatouille
Barbecue

We'll get there
In spite of ourselves

Go Down Moses

When Israel was in Egypt's land
Let my people go
Oppress'd so hard they could not stand
Let my people go

Go down, Moses
Way down in Egypt's land
Tell old Pharaoh
Let my people go

The Lord, by Moses, to Pharaoh said: Oh! let my people go
If not, I'll smite your first-born dead—Oh! let my people go
Oh! go down, Moses
Away down to Egypt's land
And tell King Pharaoh
To let my people go

TRADITIONAL SPIRITUAL

Once
We dreamed
Of making love
And supper
In the same old afternoon
Laughing at nothing
And everything
Singing the silliest songs
Happy enough to
Celebrate the earth
And us

Now
We've poisoned the air
Apparently
With our wars

And tribal animosities

Once again
Guns and ammunition
Invade
The bourgeois world
Of WalMart
Mortgages
And student debt

Oh! Let my people go

That means you
White
Black
Latinex
Indigenous
Let's not forget red dot Indians
The Lebanese
The Mung
The Nicaraguans
And anyone else
Who needs to breathe

Oh! Let my people go

That's me
Overloaded with myself
When all I really want
Is love
Just like our songs
Have been telling us
In between
The shootings
And the burials

Labels
Categories
Innuendo
Turn us inside out
Creating rank mythologies
Who's stupid
Who deserves to rule
Who's got the money . . .

Oh! Let my people go

World War II

World War II or the Second World War was a global war that lasted from 1939 to 1945. It involved all of the great powers, with more than 100 million personnel from more than 30 countries.

"World War II," Wikipedia

The Holocaust hovers
Even here
The ancestral dead
Persist like radium
A half-life of 1600 years
Iwo Jima
Guadalcanal
Bataan
D-Day Landing
Normandy
Remagen
Pearl Harbor
Auschwitz
The Rape of Nanking
Various battlefields
For high-minded barbarian pursuits
And unyielding tragedies

How many destroyers lie under the waves?
How many subs imploding?
How many thousands of small-town memorials
Plaques
Obits
Officers on horseback paralyzed in bronze?

How many crosses
Stars of David
Crescents and stars
Decorate our dead?

In the face of 800,000 funerals
The mind goes blank
The heart grows numb

Dying for one's country
For freedom
For democracy
Or maybe the king
How about the pope
How about the caliphate
Don't forget states' rights
Expiration dates abound

Dying in battle
The ultimate self-sacrifice
The most noble good
Who made that up?

Where do investors figure in this argument?
International financiers
Industrialists
Ford
The Krupps
BMW
Nestle
Porsche
Mitsubishi
Volkswagen
Bofors
IBM
Cut to the chase:
All businesses
Economies
Portfolios

Money is but energy
Like God
Like Love
Like Nagasaki
And Hiroshima

After more than a hundred million people dead
In the century just departed

In South Carolina
Home to Indian wars
Insurrections
Revolution
Lynchings
Civil War
And infinite possibility

The children ask
Where are we now?

DEEP RIVER

My home is over Jordan.
Deep river, Lord.
I want to cross over into campground.
Deep River,
My home is over Jordan.
Deep river, Lord,
I want to cross over into campground.
Oh, don't you want to go,
To the Gospel feast;
That Promised Land,
Where all is peace?
Oh, deep river, Lord,
I want to cross over into campground.

TRADITIONAL SPIRITUAL

Everybody knows
Spirituals are
Cryptograms
Secret codes
For the enslaved

Crossing the river
Going home
Angels comin'
That means now
Not then
Now
Translated
Get me out of here

We listen to the language
Bow our heads
Rumble to the rhythm
Yea Lord

Boom

Generations
Drowning
In disgrace
Black and White
Overwhelmed
By freedom
Buried in concrete
Under the Interstate

Black and white
A metaphor
For shame

We have memorized the code
We will be arriving soon
With AK-47s and Kalashnikovs

Just kidding
Sure

We know the odds

Everyone else can enjoy their glorious revolts
Just ask the DAR
Have another canape

We
On the other hand
Will work within the system

Won't we now?

CAMDEN

C AMDEN is the county seat of Kershaw County, South Carolina. Camden is known as the oldest inland city in the state; it's the capital of steeplechase.

"Camden, South Carolina," Wikipedia

In Rectory Square
Confederate cannons
Are pointed north

Gallows humor
Comes with too many coffins
To count
Hoping the honored dead can laugh

Each cannon represents a general
Born and raised right here
Kennedy
Kershaw
Cantey
Villepigue

Why did they fight
To own slaves
And then insist
The war was all about states' rights?

We know the rhetoric
We understand the arguments
We memorize complaints

Poetry becomes the quarrel with oneself
Except we have no quarrel here
Only with Northerners
And abolitionists
Who never read St. Paul

Slaves obey your masters

That's it
That's the truth
Revealed

Take the money and run
Or die destitute

You fools

STATUES

General Lee
What you doin' there
On that platform paralyzed
Bigger than life
Dressed up in bronze?

You are triumphant even in defeat
Looking down on the rest of us

By the way
How much did that statue cost?

First time ever
History dictated
By the also-rans

Let's warehouse you in some back room
Behind the Confederate battle flag
Along with the ashes of Simon Legree

And abandon the argument
Of why six hundred thousand died
Fighting for and against
The right to own slaves
You say states' rights
Okay fine
Have it your way Baby
This time
You're goin' down

Could we maybe make a statue
To honor
Choose from one below:
Thomas Edison

Nikola Tesla
George Washington Carver
Billie Holliday
How about Jonas Salk
Duke Ellington
George Gershwin
Irving Berlin
Even Aretha
Someone who brightened our days
And made us glad to be alive
Booker T. Washington
Fred Astaire
Albert Einstein
Frederick Douglass
Enrico Caruso
Steve Jobs
Don't have to be Southern
Or even American
Human will do it
Human with a heart
And maybe a brain
Let's stick with heart
Something you don't got
For all your so-called gallantry
Gallons of blood
And splattered brains
All for the holiness of
What?

Virginia?

In Jesus name

Amen

My History

Please don't take those statues down
That's my Southern history
Cried the Anglo-Saxon gentleman
Forgetting that particular demography
Was more Black than White
When cannons roared
And bodies fell down dead
And slaves bled red

Forgetting
The indentured servants
Debtors
N'er do wells
Who escaped the workhouses
Of London and
Liverpool
Forgetting
The peasants who bred him
And made him American

Forgetting the chain gangs
The dirt farms
The maternal mortality
Pellagra
Typhoid
Cholera

How could misery
Be remembered by a warrior in bronze?

How do you socialize a cracker?
Full disclosure: I'm one of them

As the nouveau riche tycoon once said
I don't believe in anything
Before sliced bread

Let us begin again
With all men created equal
Black white purple blue
However you appear
You are welcome here

Barbarians in bronze
Begone

Let us love and be loved
Like on the greeting cards
And let go of warriors

We let go of George the Third
Hapsburgs
Romanoffs
Medicis

Surely
We can let go of
The Confederacy

An idea that didn't work

And once again

Begin

Carolina in the Morning

Nothing could be finer
Than to be in Carolina
In the morning
No one could be sweeter
Than my sweetie when I meet her
In the morning
When the morning glories
Twine around the door
Whispering pretty stories
I long to hear once more
Strolling with my girlie
Where the dew is pearly early
In the morning
Butterflies all flutter up
And kiss each little buttercup
At dawning
If I had Aladdin's lamp
For only a day
I'd make a wish
And here's what I'd say
Nothing could be finer
Than to be in Carolina
In the morning

GUS KAHN AND WALTER DONALDSON, 1922

The tribal wars have ended
The Cherokee
The Shawnees
The Catawbas
Long since gone

We have moved past
Immovable identities
Low Country Barbadian
Upstate Irish

286

Huguenots
Even Lebanese
And the Armenians
Have blended in

Everywhere
Come Northerners
New York
Ohio

Immigrants
From India
Punjabi
Tamil
Join Mexicans from Vera Cruz
Hondurans
Guatemalans
The world is here

Watching everyone
Are the descendants
Of violated Africans
Proud
and growing stronger by the hour

We are a new people
A new configuration
A fantasy fulfilled

We mourn the death
Of an order
That could not be sustained
By a supremacy
Built on sand

Cofitachequi
Moves through the shadows
Of the loblolly pines

The ghost of
Francis Marion
The Swamp Fox patriot
Appears

What remains
Is the staggering splendor
Of the Congaree
The Edisto
The Broad

And a people
Who define themselves
By wit
By elegance
And a beauty handed down

Brown Versus Board of Education

Brown v. Board of Education of Topeka, 347 U.S. 483, was a landmark decision of the U.S. Supreme Court in which the Court ruled that U.S. state laws establishing racial segregation in public schools are unconstitutional, even if the segregated schools are otherwise equal in quality.

"Brown v Board of Education," Wikipedia

Why are we Americans
The only folk
So far
In this so-called civilized world
That fixates on Black and White?

Or maybe not.
Were the Brits any better?
Or the Belgians?
Hey!
What about Johannesburg?

At what point
Is a glamorous tan
Considered
Too dark
For the country club?
When does curly hair
Pass the point of no return?

When was the dividing line
In the human soul foretold?

Where is the one drop rule
In the mind of the Creator God?
When did Black and White
Diverge
Where children are concerned?

Open your eyes
Black can be
Copper
And sometimes gold

What we call white
Wanders into pink
Yellow
Beige

And sometimes beige encounters beige
And calls it Black
And or maybe White

Or What?

Joshua Fit the Battle of Jericho

E ARLY versions include the dialect word, "fit" for "fought." The lyrics recall the biblical story of the Battle of Jericho, where Joshua led the Israelites against Canaan (Joshua 6:15–21). The words also suggest the eventual escape from slavery.

"Joshua Fit the Battle of Jericho," Wikipedia

> *Joshua fit the battle of Jericho*
> *Jericho*
> *Joshua fit the battle of Jericho*
> *And the walls come tumbling down*
>
> *God knows that*
> *Joshua fit the battle of Jericho*
> *Jericho*
> *Joshua fit the battle of Jericho*
> *And the walls come tumbling down*

TRADITIONAL SPIRITUAL

Joshua fit the Battle of Jericho
Oh sure
And the walls came tumblin' down
That's right
Definitely cathode ray technology
The power of sound
Joshua an off-planet extraterrestrial

We could have used him
At Vicksburg
Fort Donelson
Gettysburg
Chattanooga
Chickamauga
Appomattox
Otherwise

Why would we
Celebrate that victory now?

The overriding energy of slavery
Infects the air
Even now
Speaking of coded language
In South Carolina spirituals

But what about the energy of war?

Even in church
We pray to Yahweh
Ostensibly
I Am Who Am
Still the God of War
And retribution

In the Middle East
And everywhere
Come worshippers with guns
Battles raging still
After five millennia

Football has never been
The perfect substitute for war

When slavery stopped
It came with the stroke of a pen
The war came afterwards

How could we live without fighting?
Our battles have given us ground
For our most immortal literature
And our Academy Awards:
Heroes on horseback
Triumphant tragedies
Our loudest arias

Blood
Thunder
And the wrecking
Of bodies and souls

The beat goes on
The walls come tumbling down
A thousand times

Only to be built again

Amen

STROM THURMOND

J AMES Strom Thurmond Sr. (1902–2003) was an American politician, military
officer, and attorney who represented South Carolina in the United States
Senate from 1954 to 2003. Prior to his 48 years as a senator, he served as the 103rd
governor of South Carolina from 1947 to 1951.

"Strom Thurmond," Wikipedia;
"Essie Mae Washington-Williams," Wikipedia

When he was 23
And still at home
He impregnated
Ms. Carrie Butler
The family maid
African American
15
16
Something like that
Evoking centuries of
Southern gentlemen
And their non-consensual paramours

Essie Mae Washington-Williams
Was born
According to some
The secret daughter of shame
Except
She saw things differently

As Governor
Senator
South Carolina patriarch
Mr. Strom
Fought integration
And civil rights

Still in the senate at 98
99
100
Reinforcing the ancient order
Of Anglo-Saxon warriors

Essie Mae waited until afterwards
To announce herself
Only to be pilloried
For not exposing her father years before

She explained she was not raised
To disclose her family business

Her chronicle was hers
It did not belong to those
Who knew better

The story spoke for itself
For Carrie Butler
And for the several layers of truth
We often call reality

In the end
Essie Mae Washington-Williams
Owned her narrative

Her account was hers alone
It did not belong to those
Who knew better

THE SOUTH

I keep saying I love it here
South Carolina
State of grace
Warmest people in the book
That's right

My brother down from DC
Disagrees
He says it's the Fifties here
Reactionary
Obsolete

One thing's for sure
We got rivers full of
Bass, crappie, catfish, trout
Fields of quail, dove, turkey, grouse
427 species ready to go
What else you need to know?

Our horses are magnificent
Lord, forgive our greed
Forgive our stubbornness
We are ghosts desperate
For compliant flesh

Forgive ourselves
Forgive the North
Forgive the federal government
The Union dead
Lie underground

We still fight the Civil War
North South pick your direction
Desperation occupies our DNA

Yes, Ma'am.

Otherwise
To tell the truth
We are beset
With detractors
Mostly from the North

They say
Our roads disintegrate
We're poor
Unschooled
We beat our wives
Unions are unwelcome here

Otherwise
To tell the truth
We are souls unbowed

After centuries
Of suffering and survival
We celebrate the hills
The streams
The harvest
And most of all
Ourselves

We welcome the stranger
And embrace the beaten-down

Our arms are open
Our hearts are full

Come down for a day
Or two

Remember to stay
For the rest of your life

You will

In the Garden

I n *the Garden*, the favorite hymn of many South Carolinians, might be a good
place to end this conversation—at least for a time.

> *I come to the garden alone,*
> *While the dew is still on the roses,*
> *And the voice I hear falling on my ear*
> *The Son of God discloses.*
> *Refrain:*
> *And He walks with me, and He talks with me,*
> *And He tells me I am His own;*
> *And the joy we share as we tarry there,*
> *None other has ever known.*
> *He speaks, and the sound of His voice*
> *Is so sweet the birds hush their singing,*
> *And the melody that He gave to me*
> *Within my heart is ringing.*
> *I'd stay in the garden with Him,*
> *Though the night around me be falling,*
> *But He bids me go; through the voice of woe*
> *His voice to me is calling.*

CHARLES A. MILES (1913)

I come to the garden alone
Hoping for stillness
Listening for voices that never come

Even the certifiably insane
Have companions
Dead or alive
To walk with them
And talk with them
And tell them they are their own

No one bids me go
But me alone

The melody I hear
I patched together piecemeal
From the clatter of the street
And the cries of my own heart
Roses are the least of it

I make music
So I can sing
Flat
Sharp
Out of tune
However you like
Whoever you are

Somewhere
You will say
I walked with you
And talked to you
You told me I am your own

In the meantime
It's definitely a one-way street
Isn't it?

More like an abyss

Where cacti grow

And owls stand guard against the night

Amen

www.ingramcontent.com/pod-product-compliance
Lightning Source LLC
Chambersburg PA
CBHW070557270326
41926CB00013B/2348